The Importance
of Being Earnest

The Importance of Being Earnest

Oscar Wilde

Edited by John Lancaster

Series Editor: Judith Baxter

CAMBRIDGE
UNIVERSITY PRESS

PUBLISHED BY THE PRESS SYNDICATE OF THE UNIVERSITY OF CAMBRIDGE
The Pitt Building, Trumpington Street, Cambridge CB2 1RP, United Kingdom

CAMBRIDGE UNIVERSITY PRESS
The Edinburgh Building, Cambridge CB2 2RU, United Kingdom
40 West 20th Street, New York, NY 10011-4211, USA
10 Stamford Road, Oakleigh, Melbourne 3166, Australia

This edition first published 1999

Printed in the United Kingdom at the University Press, Cambridge

Typeset in Sabon and Meta

A catalogue record for this book is available from the British Library

ISBN 0 521 63952 2 paperback

Prepared for publication by Stenton Associates

CONTENTS

———————————— ✦ ————————————

CAMBRIDGE LITERATURE

This edition of *The Importance of Being Earnest* is part of the Cambridge Literature series, and has been specially prepared for students in schools and colleges who are studying the play as part of their English course.

This study edition invites you to think about what happens when you read the play, and it suggests that you are not passively responding to words on the page which have only one agreed interpretation, but that you are actively exploring and making new sense of what you read and act out. Your 'reading' will partly stem from you as an individual, from your own experiences and point of view, and to this extent your interpretation will be distinctively your own. But your reading will also stem from the fact that you belong to a culture and a community, rooted in a particular time and place. So, your understanding may have much in common with that of others in your class or study group.

There is a parallel between the way you read this play and the way it was written. The Resource Notes are devised to help you to investigate the complex nature of the writing and dramatisation process. The Resource Notes begin with the playwright's first ideas and sources of inspiration, move through to the stages of writing, publication and stage production, and end with the play's reception by the audience, reviewers, critics and students. So the general approach to study focuses on five key questions:

Who has written *The Importance of Being Earnest* and why?
The main events in Wilde's life
What type of text is *The Importance of Being Earnest*?
How was *The Importance of Being Earnest* produced?
How does the play present its subject?
Who reads/watches the play? How do they interpret it?

The text of *The Importance of Being Earnest* is presented complete and uninterrupted. Some words in the play have been glossed as they may be unfamiliar due to particular cultural or linguistic significance. The Resource Notes encourage you to take an active and imaginative approach to studying both the book and the play in and out of the classroom. As well as providing you with information about many aspects of *The Importance of Being Earnest*, they offer a wide choice of activities to work on individually, or in groups. Above all, they give you the chance to explore this witty play in a variety of ways: as a reader, an actor, a researcher, a critic and a writer.   *Judith Baxter*

INTRODUCTION

The Importance of Being Earnest was first performed on 14 February 1895. It was an immediate success, lavishly praised by most reviewers and delighting London theatre-goers. Oscar Wilde's previous play, *An Ideal Husband*, had opened on 3 January to equally rapturous acclaim. Having two immensely successful plays, running simultaneously, was the culmination of Wilde's campaign to conquer the London stage that had begun only three years previously with the production of *Lady Windermere's Fan*.

In May 1895 Wilde was sentenced to two years' imprisonment with hard labour (the maximum sentence) for various homosexual offences. He died in Paris in 1900.

Wilde's meteoric rise and equally dramatic fall were the products of publicity. His success and failure took their shape from the beginnings of mass media at the end of the nineteenth century, specifically the growth of popular newspapers and magazines. Before his success as a playwright, Wilde was, like many celebrities today, famous simply for being famous: his outrageous clothes and hairstyles were written about in magazines; his scandalously unconventional views on just about everything were quoted and discussed; his scintillating wit made him a much sought-after guest at parties and balls. But then, as so often happens today, the public's delight in being shocked by a celebrity's outrageous behaviour turned immediately to a vindictive loathing when the celebrity stepped beyond the permissible.

✦ *Activities*

1 The American painter, film-maker and manic self-publicist Andy Warhol said in 1968, 'In the future everybody will be world famous for fifteen minutes.'

a Who in the last few months has been given such brief fame, especially by the tabloids?

b Can you think of celebrities recently who have been hounded by the media because of some scandal or crime? Are any of them serious writers or artists?

2 Wilde became famous because of his wit:

'In married life three is company and two none.'

'I can resist everything except temptation.'

'Work is the curse of the drinking classes.'

'Children begin by loving their parents; after a time they judge them; rarely, if ever, do they forgive them.'

Any dictionary of quotations will have a large selection of Wilde's witticisms. Before reading this play it would be useful to read a selection and think about the following:

a Wilde said he was the kind of artist 'whose work depends on the intensification of personality'.

What do you think are the key features of Wilde's personality as projected in the quotations?

Can you think of any modern writer or artist who depends on a personality cult?

b Henry James (1843–1916), an American novelist, complained that all Wilde's characters 'talk equally strained Oscar'. In his conversation, as recorded in friends' memoirs, he often sounds like a character from one of his plays.

What are the characteristics of the Wildean speech style that make it sound formal and non-conversational? In pairs, experiment with reading these quotations aloud in different ways.

The Importance of Being Earnest

A Trivial Comedy for Serious People

THE CAST

Note that in the following cast list the words which appear in bold type are the names by which the characters are identified in the dialogue.

John Worthing, J.P. (**Jack**)
Algernon Moncrieff
Rev. Canon **Chasuble**, D.D.
Merriman, *Butler*
Lane, *Manservant*
Lady Bracknell
Hon. **Gwendolen** Fairfax
Cecily Cardew
Miss Prism, *Governess*

THE SCENES OF THE PLAY

Act 1: Algernon Moncrieff's flat in Half-Moon Street, W.

Act 2: The garden at the Manor House, Woolton

Act 3: Morning-room at the Manor House, Woolton

First Act

Scene: Morning-room in Algernon's flat in Half-Moon Street.◇ The room is luxuriously and artistically furnished. The sound of a piano is heard in the adjoining room. Lane is arranging afternoon tea on the table, and after the music has ceased, Algernon enters.

ALGERNON Did you hear what I was playing, Lane?

LANE I didn't think it polite to listen, sir.

ALGERNON I'm sorry for that, for your sake. I don't play accurately – anyone can play accurately – but I play with wonderful expression. As far as the piano is concerned, sentiment is my forte. I keep science for Life.

LANE Yes, sir.

ALGERNON And, speaking of the science of Life, have you got the cucumber sandwiches cut for Lady Bracknell?

LANE Yes, sir. (*Hands them on a salver.*)

ALGERNON (*Inspects them, takes two, and sits down on the sofa.*) Oh! ... by the way, Lane, I see from your book that on Thursday night, when Lord Shoreman and Mr Worthing were dining with me, eight bottles of champagne are entered as having been consumed.

LANE Yes, sir; eight bottles and a pint.

ALGERNON Why is it that at a bachelor's establishment the servants invariably drink the champagne? I ask merely for information.

LANE I attribute it to the superior quality of the wine, sir. I have often observed that in married households the champagne is rarely of a first-rate brand.

ALGERNON Good heavens! Is marriage so demoralising as that?

LANE I believe it *is* a very pleasant state, sir. I have had very little experience of it myself up to the present. I have only been married once. That was in consequence of a misunderstanding between myself and a young person.

ALGERNON (*Languidly.*) I don't know that I am much interested in your family life, Lane.

LANE No, sir; it is not a very interesting subject. I never think of it myself.

ALGERNON Very natural, I am sure. That will do, Lane, thank you.

LANE Thank you, sir.

    Lane goes out.

ALGERNON Lane's views on marriage seem somewhat lax. Really, if the lower orders don't set us a good example, what on earth is the use of them? They seem, as a class, to have absolutely no sense of moral responsibility.

    Enter Lane.

LANE Mr Ernest Worthing.

    Enter Jack. Lane goes out.

ALGERNON How are you, my dear Ernest? What brings you up to town?

JACK Oh, pleasure, pleasure! What else should bring one anywhere? Eating as usual, I see, Algy!

ALGERNON (*Stiffly.*) I believe it is customary in good society to take some slight refreshment at five o'clock.⁂ Where have you been since last Thursday?

JACK (*Sitting down on the sofa.*) In the country.

ALGERNON What on earth do you do there?

JACK (*Pulling off his gloves.*) When one is in town one amuses oneself. When one is in the country one amuses other people. It is excessively boring.

ALGERNON And who are the people you amuse?

JACK (*Airily*.) Oh, neighbours, neighbours.

ALGERNON Got nice neighbours in your part of Shropshire?

JACK Perfectly horrid! Never speak to one of them.

ALGERNON How immensely you must amuse them! (*Goes over and takes sandwich*.) By the way, Shropshire is your county, is it not?

JACK Eh? Shropshire? Yes, of course. Hallo! Why all these cups? Why cucumber sandwiches? Why such reckless extravagance in one so young? Who is coming to tea?

ALGERNON Oh! merely Aunt Augusta and Gwendolen.

JACK How perfectly delightful!

ALGERNON Yes, that is all very well; but I am afraid Aunt Augusta won't quite approve of your being here.

JACK May I ask why?

ALGERNON My dear fellow, the way you flirt with Gwendolen is perfectly disgraceful. It is almost as bad as the way Gwendolen flirts with you.

JACK I am in love with Gwendolen. I have come up to town expressly to propose to her.

ALGERNON I thought you had come up for pleasure? ... I call that business.

JACK How utterly unromantic you are!

ALGERNON I really don't see anything romantic in proposing. It is very romantic to be in love. But there is nothing romantic about a definite proposal. Why, one may be accepted. One usually is, I believe. Then the excitement is all over. The very essence of romance is uncertainty. If ever I get married, I'll certainly try to forget the fact.

JACK I have no doubt about that, dear Algy. The Divorce Court was specially invented for people whose memories are so curiously constituted.

ALGERNON Oh! there is no use speculating on that subject. Divorces are made in Heaven – (*Jack puts out his hand to take a sandwich. Algernon at once interferes.*) Please don't touch the cucumber sandwiches. They are ordered specially for Aunt Augusta. (*Takes one and eats it.*)

JACK Well, you have been eating them all the time.

ALGERNON That is quite a different matter. She is my aunt. (*Takes plate from below.*) Have some bread and butter. The bread and butter is for Gwendolen. Gwendolen is devoted to bread and butter.

JACK (*Advancing to table and helping himself.*) And very good bread and butter it is too.

ALGERNON Well, my dear fellow, you need not eat as if you were going to eat it all. You behave as if you were married to her already. You are not married to her already, and I don't think you ever will be.

JACK Why on earth do you say that?

ALGERNON Well, in the first place girls never marry the men they flirt with. Girls don't think it right.

JACK Oh, that is nonsense!

ALGERNON It isn't. It is a great truth. It accounts for the extraordinary number of bachelors that one sees all over the place. In the second place, I don't give my consent.

JACK Your consent!

ALGERNON My dear fellow, Gwendolen is my first cousin. And before I allow you to marry her, you will have to clear up the whole question of Cecily. (*Rings bell.*)

JACK Cecily! What on earth do you mean? What do you mean, Algy, by Cecily! I don't know anyone of the name of Cecily.

    Enter Lane.

ALGERNON Bring me that cigarette case Mr Worthing left in the smoking-room the last time he dined here.

LANE Yes, sir.

Lane goes out.

JACK Do you mean to say you have had my cigarette case all this time? I wish to goodness you had let me know. I have been writing frantic letters to Scotland Yard about it. I was very nearly offering a large reward.

ALGERNON Well, I wish you would offer one. I happen to be more than usually hard up.

JACK There is no good offering a large reward now that the thing is found.

Enter Lane with the cigarette case on a salver.
Algernon takes it at once. Lane goes out.

ALGERNON I think that is rather mean of you, Ernest, I must say. (*Opens case and examines it.*) However, it makes no matter, for, now that I look at the inscription inside, I find that the thing isn't yours after all.

JACK Of course it's mine. (*Moving to him.*) You have seen me with it a hundred times, and you have no right whatsoever to read what is written inside. It is a very ungentlemanly thing to read a private cigarette case.

ALGERNON Oh! it is absurd to have a hard and fast rule about what one should read and what one shouldn't. More than half of modern culture depends on what one shouldn't read.

JACK I am quite aware of the fact, and I don't propose to discuss modern culture. It isn't the sort of thing one should talk of in private. I simply want my cigarette case back.

ALGERNON Yes; but this isn't your cigarette case. This cigarette case is a present from some one of the name of Cecily, and you said you didn't know any one of that name.

JACK Well, if you want to know, Cecily happens to be my aunt.

ALGERNON Your aunt!

JACK Yes. Charming old lady she is, too. Lives at Tunbridge Wells.* Just give it back to me, Algy.

ALGERNON (*Retreating to back of sofa.*) But why does she call herself little Cecily if she is your aunt and lives at Tunbridge Wells? (*Reading.*) 'From little Cecily with her fondest love.'

JACK (*Moving to sofa and kneeling upon it.*) My dear fellow, what on earth is there in that? Some aunts are tall, some aunts are not tall. That is a matter that surely an aunt may be allowed to decide for herself. You seem to think that every aunt should be exactly like your aunt! That is absurd. For Heaven's sake give me back my cigarette case. (*Follows Algernon round the room.*)

ALGERNON Yes. But why does your aunt call you her uncle? 'From little Cecily, with her fondest love to her dear Uncle Jack.' There is no objection, I admit, to an aunt being a small aunt, but why an aunt, no matter what her size may be, should call her own nephew her uncle, I can't quite make out. Besides, your name isn't Jack at all; it is Ernest.

JACK It isn't Ernest; it's Jack.

ALGERNON You have always told me it was Ernest. I have introduced you to everyone as Ernest. You answer to the name of Ernest. You look as if your name was Ernest. You are the most earnest-looking person I ever saw in my life. It is perfectly absurd your saying that your name isn't Ernest. It's on your cards. Here is one of them. (*Taking it from case.*) 'Mr Ernest Worthing, B.4, The Albany.' I'll keep this as a proof that your name is Ernest if ever you attempt to deny it to me, or to Gwendolen, or to anyone else. (*Puts the card in his pocket.*)

JACK Well, my name is Ernest in town and Jack in the country, and the cigarette case was given to me in the country.

ALGERNON Yes, but that does not account for the fact that your small Aunt Cecily, who lives at Tunbridge Wells, calls you her dear uncle. Come, old boy, you had much better have the thing out at once.

JACK My dear Algy, you talk exactly as if you were a dentist. It is very vulgar to talk like a dentist when one isn't a dentist. It produces a false impression.

ALGERNON Well, that is exactly what dentists always do. Now, go on! Tell me the whole thing. I may mention that I have always suspected you of being a confirmed and secret Bunburyist; and I am quite sure of it now.

JACK Bunburyist? What on earth do you mean by a Bunburyist?

ALGERNON I'll reveal to you the meaning of that incomparable expression as soon as you are kind enough to inform me why you are Ernest in town and Jack in the country.

JACK Well, produce my cigarette case first.

ALGERNON Here it is. (*Hands cigarette case.*) Now produce your explanation, and pray make it improbable. (*Sits on sofa.*)

JACK My dear fellow, there is nothing improbable about my explanation at all. In fact it's perfectly ordinary. Old Mr Thomas Cardew, who adopted me when I was a little boy, made me in his will guardian to his grand-daughter, Miss Cecily Cardew. Cecily, who addresses me as her uncle from motives of respect that you could not possibly appreciate, lives at my place in the country under the charge of her admirable governess, Miss Prism.

ALGERNON Where is that place in the country, by the way?

JACK That is nothing to you, dear boy. You are not going to be invited. ... I may tell you candidly that the place is not in Shropshire.

ALGERNON I suspected that, my dear fellow! I have Bunburyed all over Shropshire on two separate occasions. Now, go on. Why are you Ernest in town and Jack in the country?

JACK My dear Algy, I don't know whether you will be able to understand my real motives. You are hardly serious enough. When one is placed in the position of guardian, one has to adopt a very high moral tone on all subjects. It's one's duty to do so. And as a high moral tone can hardly be said to conduce very much to either one's health or one's happiness, in order to get up to town I have always pretended to have a younger brother of the name of Ernest, who lives in the Albany, and gets into the most dreadful scrapes. That, my dear Algy, is the whole truth pure and simple.

ALGERNON The truth is rarely pure and never simple. Modern life would be very tedious if it were either, and modern literature a complete impossibility!

JACK That wouldn't be at all a bad thing.

ALGERNON Literary criticism is not your forte, my dear fellow. Don't try it. You should leave that to people who haven't been at a University. They do it so well in the daily papers. What you really are is a Bunburyist. I was quite right in saying you were a Bunburyist. You are one of the most advanced Bunburyists I know.

JACK What on earth do you mean?

ALGERNON You have invented a very useful younger
brother called Ernest, in order that you may be able
to come up to town as often as you like. I have
invented an invaluable permanent invalid called
Bunbury, in order that I may be able to go down
into the country whenever I choose. Bunbury is
perfectly invaluable. If it wasn't for Bunbury's
extraordinary bad health, for instance, I wouldn't be
able to dine with you at Willis's° to-night, for I have
been really engaged to Aunt Augusta for more than
a week.

JACK I haven't asked you to dine with me anywhere
to-night.

ALGERNON I know. You are absurdly careless about
sending out invitations. It is very foolish of you.
Nothing annoys people so much as not receiving
invitations.

JACK You had much better dine with your Aunt
Augusta.

ALGERNON I haven't the smallest intention of doing
anything of the kind. To begin with, I dined there
on Monday, and once a week is quite enough to
dine with one's own relations. In the second place,
whenever I do dine there I am always treated as a
member of the family, and sent down° with either
no woman at all, or two. In the third place, I know
perfectly well whom she will place me next to,
to-night. She will place me next Mary Farquhar,
who always flirts with her own husband across the
dinner-table. That is not very pleasant. Indeed, it is
not even decent ... and that sort of thing is
enormously on the increase. The amount of women
in London who flirt with their own husbands is
perfectly scandalous. It looks so bad. It is simply
washing one's clean linen in public. Besides, now

that I know you to be a confirmed Bunburyist I naturally want to talk to you about Bunburying. I want to tell you the rules.

Jack I'm not a Bunburyist at all. If Gwendolen accepts me, I am going to kill my brother, indeed I think I'll kill him in any case. Cecily is a little too much interested in him. It is rather a bore. So I am going to get rid of Ernest. And I strongly advise you to do the same with Mr … with your invalid friend who has the absurd name.

Algernon Nothing will induce me to part with Bunbury, and if you ever get married, which seems to me extremely problematic, you will be very glad to know Bunbury. A man who marries without knowing Bunbury has a very tedious time of it.

Jack That is nonsense. If I marry a charming girl like Gwendolen, and she is the only girl I ever saw in my life that I would marry, I certainly won't want to know Bunbury.

Algernon Then your wife will. You don't seem to realise, that in married life three is company and two is none.

Jack (*Sententiously.*) That, my dear young friend, is the theory that the corrupt French Drama has been propounding for the last fifty years.

Algernon Yes; and that the happy English home has proved in half the time.

Jack For heaven's sake, don't try to be cynical. It's perfectly easy to be cynical.

Algernon My dear fellow, it isn't easy to be anything nowadays. There's such a lot of beastly competition about. (*The sound of an electric bell is heard.*) Ah! that must be Aunt Augusta. Only relatives, or creditors, ever ring in that Wagnerian° manner. Now, if I get her out of the way for ten minutes, so that you can have an opportunity for proposing to Gwendolen, may I dine with you to-night at Willis's?

JACK I suppose so, if you want to.

ALGERNON Yes, but you must be serious about it. I hate people who are not serious about meals. It is so shallow of them.

Enter Lane.

LANE Lady Bracknell and Miss Fairfax.

Algernon goes forward to meet them. Enter Lady Bracknell and Gwendolen.

LADY BRACKNELL Good afternoon, dear Algernon, I hope you are behaving very well.

ALGERNON I'm feeling very well, Aunt Augusta.

LADY BRACKNELL That's not quite the same thing. In fact the two things rarely go together. (*Sees Jack and bows to him with icy coldness.*)

ALGERNON (*To Gwendolen.*) Dear me, you are smart!

GWENDOLEN I am always smart! Am I not, Mr Worthing?

JACK You're quite perfect, Miss Fairfax.

GWENDOLEN Oh! I hope I am not that. It would leave no room for developments, and I intend to develop in many directions. (*Gwendolen and Jack sit down together in the corner.*)

LADY BRACKNELL I'm sorry if we are a little late, Algernon, but I was obliged to call on dear Lady Harbury. I hadn't been there since her poor husband's death. I never saw a woman so altered; she looks quite twenty years younger. And now I'll have a cup of tea, and one of those nice cucumber sandwiches you promised me.

ALGERNON Certainly, Aunt Augusta. (*Goes over to tea-table.*)

LADY BRACKNELL Won't you come and sit here, Gwendolen?

GWENDOLEN Thanks, mamma, I'm quite comfortable where I am.

ALGERNON (*Picking up empty plate in horror.*) Good heavens! Lane! Why are there no cucumber sandwiches? I ordered them specially.

LANE (*Gravely.*) There were no cucumbers in the market this morning, sir. I went down twice.

ALGERNON No cucumbers!

LANE No, sir. Not even for ready money.

ALGERNON That will do, Lane, thank you.

LANE Thank you, sir.

  Goes out.

ALGERNON I am greatly distressed, Aunt Augusta, about there being no cucumbers, not even for ready money.

LADY BRACKNELL It really makes no matter, Algernon. I had some crumpets with Lady Harbury, who seems to me to be living entirely for pleasure now.

ALGERNON I hear her hair has turned quite gold from grief.

LADY BRACKNELL It certainly has changed its colour. From what cause I, of course, cannot say. (*Algernon crosses and hands tea.*) Thank you. I've quite a treat for you to-night, Algernon. I am going to send you down with Mary Farquhar. She is such a nice woman, and so attentive to her husband. It's delightful to watch them.

ALGERNON I am afraid, Aunt Augusta, I shall have to give up the pleasure of dining with you to-night after all.

LADY BRACKNELL (*Frowning.*) I hope not, Algernon. It would put my table completely out. Your uncle would have to dine upstairs. Fortunately he is accustomed to that.

ALGERNON It is a great bore, and, I need hardly say, a terrible disappointment to me, but the fact is I have just had a telegram to say that my poor friend Bunbury is very ill again. (*Exchanges glances with Jack.*) They seem to think I should be with him.

LADY BRACKNELL It is very strange. This Mr Bunbury seems to suffer from curiously bad health.

ALGERNON Yes; poor Bunbury is a dreadful invalid.

LADY BRACKNELL Well, I must say, Algernon, that I think it is high time that Mr Bunbury made up his mind whether he was going to live or to die. This shilly-shallying with the question is absurd. Nor do I in any way approve of the modern sympathy with invalids. I consider it morbid. Illness of any kind is hardly a thing to be encouraged in others. Health is the primary duty of life. I am always telling that to your poor uncle, but he never seems to take much notice … as far as any improvement in his ailment goes. I should be much obliged if you would ask Mr Bunbury, from me, to be kind enough not to have a relapse on Saturday, for I rely on you to arrange my music for me. It is my last reception, and one wants something that will encourage conversation, particularly at the end of the season when every one has practically said whatever they had to say, which, in most cases, was probably not much.

ALGERNON I'll speak to Bunbury, Aunt Augusta, if he is still conscious, and I think I can promise you he'll be all right by Saturday. Of course the music is a great difficulty. You see, if one plays good music, people don't listen, and if one plays bad music people don't talk. But I'll run over the programme I've drawn out, if you will kindly come into the next room for a moment.

LADY BRACKNELL Thank you, Algernon. It is very thoughtful of you. (*Rising, and following Algernon.*) I'm sure the programme will be delightful, after a few expurgations. French songs I cannot possibly allow. People always seem to think that they are improper, and either look shocked, which is vulgar, or laugh, which is worse. But German sounds a thoroughly respectable language, and indeed, I believe is so. Gwendolen, you will accompany me.

GWENDOLEN Certainly, mamma.

> *Lady Bracknell and Algernon go into the music-room, Gwendolen remains behind.*

JACK Charming day it has been, Miss Fairfax.

GWENDOLEN Pray don't talk to me about the weather, Mr Worthing. Whenever people talk to me about the weather, I always feel quite certain that they mean something else. And that makes me so nervous.

JACK I do mean something else.

GWENDOLEN I thought so. In fact, I am never wrong.

JACK And I would like to be allowed to take advantage of Lady Bracknell's temporary absence ...

GWENDOLEN I would certainly advise you to do so. Mamma has a way of coming back suddenly into a room that I have often had to speak to her about.

JACK (*Nervously.*) Miss Fairfax, ever since I met you I have admired you more than any girl ... I have ever met since ... I met you.

GWENDOLEN Yes, I am quite well aware of the fact. And I often wish that in public, at any rate, you had been more demonstrative. For me you have always had an irresistible fascination. Even before I met you I was far from indifferent to you. (*Jack looks at her in amazement.*) We live, as I hope you know, Mr Worthing, in an age of ideals. The fact is constantly mentioned in the more expensive monthly magazines, and has reached the provincial pulpits I am told; and my ideal has always been to love some one of the name of Ernest. There is something in that name that inspires absolute confidence. The moment Algernon first mentioned to me that he had a friend called Ernest, I knew I was destined to love you.

Jack You really love me, Gwendolen?

Gwendolen Passionately!

Jack Darling! You don't know how happy you've made me.

Gwendolen My own Ernest!

Jack But you don't really mean to say that you couldn't love me if my name wasn't Ernest?

Gwendolen But your name is Ernest.

Jack Yes, I know it is. But supposing it was something else? Do you mean to say you couldn't love me then?

Gwendolen (*Glibly.*) Ah! that is clearly a metaphysical speculation, and like most metaphysical speculations has very little reference at all to the actual facts of real life, as we know them.

Jack Personally, darling, to speak quite candidly, I don't much care about the name of Ernest. ... I don't think the name suits me at all.

Gwendolen It suits you perfectly. It is a divine name. It has music of its own. It produces vibrations.

Jack Well, really, Gwendolen, I must say that I think there are lots of other much nicer names. I think Jack, for instance, a charming name.

Gwendolen Jack? ... No, there is very little music in the name Jack, if any at all, indeed. It does not thrill. It produces absolutely no vibrations. ... I have known several Jacks, and they all, without exception, were more than usually plain. Besides, Jack is a notorious domesticity for John! And I pity any woman who is married to a man called John. She would probably never be allowed to know the entrancing pleasure of a single moment's solitude. The only really safe name is Ernest.

JACK Gwendolen, I must get christened at once – I mean we must get married at once. There is no time to be lost.

GWENDOLEN Married, Mr Worthing?

JACK (*Astounded.*) Well … surely. You know that I love you, and you led me to believe, Miss Fairfax, that you were not absolutely indifferent to me.

GWENDOLEN I adore you. But you haven't proposed to me yet. Nothing has been said at all about marriage. The subject has not even been touched on.

JACK Well … may I propose to you now?

GWENDOLEN I think it would be an admirable opportunity. And to spare you any possible disappointment, Mr Worthing, I think it only fair to tell you quite frankly beforehand that I am fully determined to accept you.

JACK Gwendolen!

GWENDOLEN Yes, Mr Worthing, what have you got to say to me?

JACK You know what I have got to say to you.

GWENDOLEN Yes, but you don't say it.

JACK Gwendolen, will you marry me? (*Goes on his knees.*)

GWENDOLEN Of course I will, darling. How long you have been about it! I am afraid you have had very little experience in how to propose.

JACK My own one, I have never loved anyone in the world but you.

GWENDOLEN Yes, but men often propose for practice. I know my brother Gerald does. All my girl-friends tell me so. What wonderfully blue eyes you have, Ernest! They are quite, quite, blue. I hope you will always look at me just like that, especially when there are other people present.

Enter Lady Bracknell.

LADY BRACKNELL Mr Worthing! Rise, sir, from this semi-recumbent posture. It is most indecorous.

GWENDOLEN Mamma! (*He tries to rise; she restrains him.*) I must beg you to retire. This is no place for you. Besides, Mr Worthing has not quite finished yet.

LADY BRACKNELL Finished what, may I ask?

GWENDOLEN I am engaged to Mr Worthing, mamma. (*They rise together.*)

LADY BRACKNELL Pardon me, you are not engaged to any-one. When you do become engaged to some one, I, or your father, should his health permit him, will inform you of the fact. An engagement should come on a young girl as a surprise, pleasant or unpleasant, as the case may be. It is hardly a matter that she could be allowed to arrange for herself. ... And now I have a few questions to put to you, Mr Worthing. While I am making these inquiries, you, Gwendolen, will wait for me below the carriage.

GWENDOLEN (*Reproachfully.*) Mamma!

LADY BRACKNELL In the carriage, Gwendolen!

Gwendolen goes to the door. She and Jack blow kisses to each other behind Lady Bracknell's back. Lady Bracknell looks vaguely about as if she could not understand what the noise was. Finally turns round.

Gwendolen, the carriage!

GWENDOLEN Yes, mamma.

Goes out, looking back at Jack.

LADY BRACKNELL (*Sitting down.*) You can take a seat, Mr Worthing. (*Looks in her pocket for note-book and pencil.*)

JACK Thank you, Lady Bracknell, I prefer standing.

LADY BRACKNELL (*Pencil and note-book in hand.*) I feel bound to tell you that you are not down on my list of eligible young men, although I have the same list as the dear Duchess of Bolton has. We work together, in fact. However, I am quite ready to enter your name, should your answers be what a really affectionate mother requires. Do you smoke?

JACK Well, yes, I must admit I smoke.

LADY BRACKNELL I am glad to hear it. A man should always have an occupation of some kind. There are far too many idle men in London as it is. How old are you?

JACK Twenty-nine.

LADY BRACKNELL A very good age to be married at. I have always been of opinion that a man who desires to get married should know either everything or nothing. Which do you know?

JACK (*After some hesitation.*) I know nothing, Lady Bracknell.

LADY BRACKNELL I am pleased to hear it. I do not approve of anything that tampers with natural ignorance. Ignorance is like a delicate exotic fruit; touch it and the bloom is gone. The whole theory of modern education is radically unsound. Fortunately in England, at any rate, education produces no effect whatsoever. If it did, it would prove a serious danger to the upper classes, and probably lead to acts of violence in Grosvenor Square. What is your income?

JACK Between seven and eight thousand a year.

Lady Bracknell (*Makes a note in her book.*) In land, or in investments?

Jack In investments, chiefly.

Lady Bracknell That is satisfactory. What between the duties expected of one during one's lifetime, and the duties exacted from one after one's death,° land has ceased to be either a profit or a pleasure. It gives one position, and prevents one from keeping it up. That's all that can be said about land.

Jack I have a country house with some land, of course, attached to it, about fifteen hundred acres, I believe; but I don't depend on that for my real income. In fact, as far as I can make out, the poachers are the only people who make anything out of it.

Lady Bracknell A country house! How many bedrooms? Well, that point can be cleared up afterwards. You have a town house, I hope? A girl with a simple, unspoiled nature, like Gwendolen, could hardly be expected to reside in the country.

Jack Well, I own a house in Belgrave Square, but it is let by the year to Lady Bloxham. Of course, I can get it back whenever I like, at six months' notice.

Lady Bracknell Lady Bloxham? I don't know her.

Jack Oh, she goes about very little. She is a lady considerably advanced in years.

Lady Bracknell Ah, nowadays that is no guarantee of respectability of character. What number in Belgrave Square?

Jack 149.

Lady Bracknell (*Shaking her head.*) The unfashionable side. I thought there was something. However, that could easily be altered.

Jack Do you mean the fashion, or the side?

Lady Bracknell (*Sternly.*) Both, if necessary, I presume. What are your politics?

JACK Well, I am afraid I really have none. I am a Liberal Unionist.◇

LADY BRACKNELL Oh, they count as Tories. They dine with us. Or come in the evening, at any rate. Now to minor matters. Are your parents living?

JACK I have lost both my parents.

LADY BRACKNELL To lose one parent, Mr Worthing, may be regarded as a misfortune; to lose both looks like carelessness. Who was your father? He was evidently a man of some wealth. Was he born in what the Radical papers call the purple of commerce, or did he rise from the ranks of the aristocracy?

JACK I am afraid I really don't know. The fact is, Lady Bracknell, I said I had lost my parents. It would be nearer the truth to say that my parents seem to have lost me. … I don't actually know who I am by birth. I was … well, I was found.

LADY BRACKNELL Found!

JACK The late Mr Thomas Cardew, an old gentleman of a very charitable and kindly disposition, found me, and gave me the name of Worthing, because he happened to have a first-class ticket for Worthing in his pocket at the time. Worthing is a place in Sussex. It is a seaside resort.

LADY BRACKNELL Where did the charitable gentleman who had a first-class ticket for this seaside resort find you?

JACK (*Gravely.*) In a hand-bag.

LADY BRACKNELL A hand-bag?

JACK (*Very seriously.*) Yes, Lady Bracknell. I was in a hand-bag – a somewhat large, black leather hand-bag, with handles to it – an ordinary hand-bag in fact.

Lady Bracknell In what locality did this Mr James, or Thomas, Cardew come across this ordinary hand-bag?

Jack In the cloak-room° at Victoria Station. It was given to him in mistake for his own.

Lady Bracknell The cloak-room at Victoria Station?

Jack Yes. The Brighton line.

Lady Bracknell The line is immaterial. Mr Worthing, I confess I feel somewhat bewildered by what you have just told me. To be born, or at any rate bred, in a hand-bag, whether it had handles or not, seems to me to display a contempt for the ordinary decencies of family life that reminds one of the worst excesses of the French Revolution. And, I presume you know what that unfortunate movement led to? As for the particular locality in which the hand-bag was found, a cloak-room at a railway station might serve to conceal a social indiscretion° – has probably, indeed, been used for that purpose before now – but it could hardly be regarded as an assured basis for a recognised position in good society.

Jack May I ask you then what you would advise me to do? I need hardly say I would do anything in the world to ensure Gwendolen's happiness.

Lady Bracknell I would strongly advise you, Mr Worthing, to try and acquire some relations as soon as possible, and to make a definite effort to produce at any rate one parent, of either sex, before the season° is quite over.

Jack Well, I don't see how I could possibly manage to do that. I can produce the hand-bag at any moment. It is in my dressing-room at home. I really think that should satisfy you, Lady Bracknell.

LADY BRACKNELL Me, sir! What has it to do with me? You can hardly imagine that I and Lord Bracknell would dream of allowing our only daughter – a girl brought up with the utmost care – to marry into a cloak-room, and form an alliance with a parcel. Good morning, Mr Worthing!

Lady Bracknell sweeps out in majestic indignation.

JACK Good morning! (*Algernon, from the other room, strikes up the Wedding March. Jack looks perfectly furious, and goes to the door.*) For goodness' sake don't play that ghastly tune, Algy! How idiotic you are!

The music stops and Algernon enters cheerily.

ALGERNON Didn't it go off all right, old boy? You don't mean to say Gwendolen refused you? I know it is a way she has. She is always refusing people. I think it is most ill-natured of her.

JACK Oh, Gwendolen is as right as a trivet. As far as she is concerned, we are engaged. Her mother is perfectly unbearable. Never met such a Gorgon.◊ ... I don't really know what a Gorgon is like, but I am quite sure that Lady Bracknell is one. In any case, she is a monster, without being a myth, which is rather unfair. ... I beg your pardon, Algy, I suppose I shouldn't talk about your own aunt in that way before you.

ALGERNON My dear boy, I love hearing my relations abused. It is the only thing that makes me put up with them at all. Relations are simply a tedious pack of people, who haven't got the remotest knowledge of how to live, nor the smallest instinct about when to die.

JACK Oh, that is nonsense!

ALGERNON It isn't!

JACK Well, I won't argue about the matter. You always want to argue about things.

ALGERNON That is exactly what things were originally made for.

JACK Upon my word, if I thought that, I'd shoot myself. … (*A pause.*) You don't think there is any chance of Gwendolen becoming like her mother in about a hundred and fifty years, do you, Algy?

ALGERNON All women become like their mothers. That is their tragedy. No man does. That's his.

JACK Is that clever?

ALGERNON It is perfectly phrased! and quite as true as any observation in civilised life should be.

JACK I am sick to death of cleverness. Everybody is clever nowadays. You can't go anywhere without meeting clever people. The thing has become an absolute public nuisance. I wish to goodness we had a few fools left.

ALGERNON We have.

JACK I should extremely like to meet them. What do they talk about?

ALGERNON The fools? Oh! about the clever people, of course.

JACK What fools!

ALGERNON By the way, did you tell Gwendolen the truth about your being Ernest in town, and Jack in the country?

JACK (*In a very patronising manner.*) My dear fellow, the truth isn't quite the sort of thing one tells to a nice, sweet, refined girl. What extraordinary ideas you have about the way to behave to a woman!

ALGERNON The only way to behave to a woman is to make love to her, if she is pretty, and to some one else, if she is plain.

JACK Oh, that is nonsense.

ALGERNON What about your brother? What about the profligate Ernest?

JACK Oh, before the end of the week I shall have got rid of him. I'll say he died in Paris of apoplexy. Lots of people die of apoplexy, quite suddenly, don't they?

ALGERNON Yes, but it's hereditary, my dear fellow. It's a sort of thing that runs in families. You had much better say a severe chill.

JACK You are sure a severe chill isn't hereditary, or anything of that kind?

ALGERNON Of course it isn't!

JACK Very well, then. My poor brother Ernest is carried off suddenly, in Paris, by a severe chill. That gets rid of him.

ALGERNON But I thought you said that ... Miss Cardew was a little too much interested in your poor brother Ernest? Won't she feel his loss a good deal?

JACK Oh, that is all right. Cecily is not a silly romantic girl, I am glad to say. She has got a capital appetite, goes long walks, and pays no attention at all to her lessons.

ALGERNON I would rather like to see Cecily.

JACK I will take very good care you never do. She is excessively pretty, and she is only just eighteen.⁕

ALGERNON Have you told Gwendolen yet that you have an excessively pretty ward who is only just eighteen?

JACK Oh! one doesn't blurt these things out to people. Cecily and Gwendolen are perfectly certain to be extremely great friends. I'll bet you anything you like that half an hour after they have met, they will be calling each other sister.

ALGERNON Women only do that when they have called each other a lot of other things first. Now, my dear boy, if we want to get a good table at Willis's, we really must go and dress. Do you know it is nearly seven?

JACK (*Irritably.*) Oh! it always is nearly seven.

ALGERNON Well, I'm hungry.

JACK I never knew you when you weren't. ...

ALGERNON What shall we do after dinner? Go to a theatre?

JACK Oh no! I loathe listening.

ALGERNON Well, let us go to the Club?◇

JACK Oh, no! I hate talking.

ALGERNON Well, we might trot round to the Empire◇ at ten?

JACK Oh, no! I can't bear looking at things. It is so silly.

ALGERNON Well, what shall we do?

JACK Nothing!

ALGERNON It is awfully hard work doing nothing. However, I don't mind hard work where there is no definite object of any kind.

Enter Lane.

LANE Miss Fairfax.

Enter Gwendolen. Lane goes out.

ALGERNON Gwendolen, upon my word!

GWENDOLEN Algy, kindly turn your back. I have something very particular to say to Mr Worthing.

ALGERNON Really, Gwendolen, I don't think I can allow this at all.

GWENDOLEN Algy, you always adopt a strictly immoral attitude towards life. You are not quite old enough to do that. (*Algernon retires to the fireplace.*)

JACK My own darling!

GWENDOLEN Ernest, we may never be married. From the expression on mamma's face I fear we never shall. Few parents nowadays pay any regard to what their children say to them. The old-fashioned respect for the young is fast dying out. Whatever influence I ever had over mamma, I lost at the age of three. But although she may prevent us from becoming man and wife, and I may marry some one else, and marry often, nothing that she can possibly do can alter my eternal devotion to you.

JACK Dear Gwendolen!

GWENDOLEN The story of your romantic origin, as related to me by mamma, with unpleasing comments, has naturally stirred the deeper fibres of my nature. Your Christian name has an irresistible fascination. The simplicity of your character makes you exquisitely incomprehensible to me. Your town address at the Albany I have. What is your address in the country?

JACK The Manor House, Woolton, Hertfordshire.

Algernon, who has been carefully listening, smiles to himself, and writes the address on his shirt-cuff. Then picks up the Railway Guide.

GWENDOLEN There is a good postal service, I suppose? It may be necessary to do something desperate. That of course will require serious consideration. I will communicate with you daily.

JACK My own one!

GWENDOLEN How long do you remain in town?

JACK Till Monday.

GWENDOLEN Good! Algy, you may turn round now.

ALGERNON Thanks, I've turned round already.

GWENDOLEN You may also ring the bell.

JACK You will let me see you to your carriage, my own darling?

GWENDOLEN Certainly.

JACK (*To Lane, who now enters.*) I will see Miss Fairfax out.

LANE Yes, sir.

Jack and Gwendolen go off. Lane presents several letters on a salver to Algernon. It is to be surmised that they are bills, as Algernon, after looking at the envelopes, tears them up.

ALGERNON A glass of sherry, Lane.

LANE Yes, sir.

ALGERNON Tomorrow, Lane, I'm going Bunburying.

LANE Yes, sir.

ALGERNON I shall probably not be back till Monday. You can put up my dress clothes, my smoking jacket, and all the Bunbury suits. ...

LANE Yes, sir. (*Handing sherry.*)

ALGERNON I hope to-morrow will be a fine day, Lane.

LANE It never is, sir.

ALGERNON Lane, you're a perfect pessimist.

LANE I do my best to give satisfaction, sir.

Enter Jack. Lane goes off.

JACK There's a sensible, intellectual girl! the only girl I ever cared for in my life. (*Algernon is laughing immoderately.*) What on earth are you so amused at?

ALGERNON Oh, I'm a little anxious about poor Bunbury, that is all.

JACK If you don't take care, your friend Bunbury will get you into a serious scrape some day.

ALGERNON I love scrapes. They are the only things that are never serious.

JACK Oh, that's nonsense, Algy. You never talk anything but nonsense.

ALGERNON Nobody ever does.

Jack looks indignantly at him, and leaves the room. Algernon lights a cigarette, reads his shirt-cuff, and smiles.

ACT DROP

Second Act

Scene: Garden at the Manor House. A flight of grey stone steps leads up to the house. The garden, an old-fashioned one, full of roses. Time of year, July. Basket chairs, and a table covered with books, are set under a large yew-tree. Miss Prism discovered seated at the table. Cecily is at the back watering flowers.

MISS PRISM (*Calling.*) Cecily, Cecily! Surely such a utilitarian occupation as the watering of flowers is rather Moulton's duty than yours? Especially at a moment when intellectual pleasures await you. Your German grammar is on the table. Pray open it at page fifteen. We will repeat yesterday's lesson.

CECILY (*Coming over very slowly.*) But I don't like German. It isn't at all a becoming language. I know perfectly well that I look quite plain after my German lesson.

MISS PRISM Child, you know how anxious your guardian is that you should improve yourself in every way. He laid particular stress on your German, as he was leaving for town yesterday. Indeed, he always lays stress on your German when he is leaving for town.

CECILY Dear Uncle Jack is so very serious! Sometimes he is so serious that I think he cannot be quite well.

MISS PRISM (*Drawing herself up.*) Your guardian enjoys the best of health, and his gravity of demeanour is especially to be commended in one so comparatively young as he is. I know no one who has a higher sense of duty and responsibility.

CECILY I suppose that is why he often looks a little bored when we three are together.

MISS PRISM Cecily! I am surprised at you. Mr Worthing has many troubles in his life. Idle merriment and triviality would be out of place in his conversation. You must remember his constant anxiety about that unfortunate young man his brother.

CECILY I wish Uncle Jack would allow that unfortunate young man, his brother, to come down here sometimes. We might have a good influence over him, Miss Prism. I am sure you certainly would. You know German, and geology, and things of that kind influence a man very much. (*Cecily begins to write in her diary.*)

MISS PRISM (*Shaking her head.*) I do not think that even I could produce any effect on a character that according to his own brother's admission is irretrievably weak and vacillating. Indeed I am not sure that I would desire to reclaim him. I am not in favour of this modern mania for turning bad people into good people at a moment's notice. As a man sows so let him reap. You must put away your diary, Cecily. I really don't see why you should keep a diary at all.

CECILY I keep a diary in order to enter the wonderful secrets of my life. If I didn't write them down, I should probably forget all about them.

MISS PRISM Memory, my dear Cecily, is the diary that we all carry about with us.

CECILY Yes, but it usually chronicles the things that have never happened, and couldn't possibly have happened. I believe that Memory is responsible for nearly all the three-volume novels that Mudie⋄ sends us.

Miss Prism Do not speak slightingly of the three-volume novel, Cecily. I wrote one myself in earlier days.

Cecily Did you really, Miss Prism? How wonderfully clever you are! I hope it did not end happily? I don't like novels that end happily. They depress me so much.

Miss Prism The good ended happily, and the bad unhappily. That is what Fiction means.

Cecily I suppose so. But it seems very unfair. And was your novel ever published?

Miss Prism Alas! no. The manuscript unfortunately was abandoned.◇ (*Cecily starts.*) I use the word in the sense of lost or mislaid. To your work, child, these speculations are profitless.

Cecily (*Smiling.*) But I see dear Dr Chasuble coming up through the garden.

Miss Prism (*Rising and advancing.*) Dr Chasuble! This is indeed a pleasure.

Enter Canon Chasuble.◇

Chasuble And how are we this morning? Miss Prism, you are, I trust, well?

Cecily Miss Prism has just been complaining of a slight headache. I think it would do her so much good to have a short stroll with you in the Park, Dr Chasuble.

Miss Prism Cecily, I have not mentioned anything about a headache.

Cecily No, dear Miss Prism, I know that, but I felt instinctively that you had a headache. Indeed I was thinking about that, and not about my German lesson, when the Rector came in.

Chasuble I hope, Cecily, you are not inattentive.

Cecily Oh, I am afraid I am.

CHASUBLE That is strange. Were I fortunate enough to be Miss Prism's pupil, I would hang upon her lips. (*Miss Prism glares.*) I spoke metaphorically. – My metaphor was drawn from bees. Ahem! Mr Worthing, I suppose, has not returned from town yet?

MISS PRISM We do not expect him till Monday afternoon.

CHASUBLE Ah yes, he usually likes to spend his Sunday in London. He is not one of those whose sole aim is enjoyment, as, by all accounts, that unfortunate young man his brother seems to be. But I must not disturb Egeria° and her pupil any longer.

MISS PRISM Egeria? My name is Laetitia,° Doctor.

CHASUBLE (*Bowing.*) A classical allusion merely, drawn from the Pagan authors. I shall see you both no doubt at Evensong?

MISS PRISM I think, dear Doctor, I will have a stroll with you. I find I have a headache after all, and a walk might do it good.

CHASUBLE With pleasure, Miss Prism, with pleasure. We might go as far as the schools and back.

MISS PRISM That would be delightful. Cecily, you will read your Political Economy in my absence. The chapter on the Fall of the Rupee you may omit. It is somewhat too sensational. Even these metallic problems have their melodramatic side.

> *Goes down the garden with Dr Chasuble.*

CECILY (*Picks up books and throws them back on table.*) Horrid Political Economy! Horrid Geography! Horrid, horrid German!

> *Enter Merriman with a card on a salver.*

MERRIMAN Mr Ernest Worthing has just driven over from the station. He has brought his luggage with him.

CECILY (*Takes the card and reads it.*) 'Mr Ernest
Worthing, B.4, The Albany, W.' Uncle Jack's
brother! Did you tell him Mr Worthing was in
town?

MERRIMAN Yes, Miss. He seemed very much
disappointed. I mentioned that you and Miss Prism
were in the garden. He said he was anxious to speak
to you privately for a moment.

CECILY Ask Mr Ernest Worthing to come here. I
suppose you had better talk to the housekeeper
about a room for him.

MERRIMAN Yes, Miss.

Merriman goes off.

CECILY I have never met any really wicked person
before. I feel rather frightened. I am so afraid he will
look just like everyone else.

Enter Algernon, very gay and debonair.

He does!

ALGERNON (*Raising his hat.*) You are my little cousin
Cecily, I'm sure.

CECILY You are under some strange mistake. I am not
little. In fact, I believe I am more than usually tall
for my age. (*Algernon is rather taken aback.*) But I
am your cousin Cecily. You, I see from your card,
are Uncle Jack's brother, my cousin Ernest, my
wicked cousin Ernest.

ALGERNON Oh! I am not really wicked at all, cousin
Cecily. You mustn't think that I am wicked.

CECILY If you are not, then you have certainly been
deceiving us all in a very inexcusable manner. I hope
you have not been leading a double life, pretending
to be wicked and being really good all the time.
That would be hypocrisy.

ALGERNON (*Looks at her in amazement.*) Oh! Of course I
have been rather reckless.

CECILY I am glad to hear it.

ALGERNON In fact, now you mention the subject, I have been very bad in my own small way.

CECILY I don't think you should be so proud of that, though I am sure it must have been very pleasant.

ALGERNON It is much pleasanter being here with you.

CECILY I can't understand how you are here at all. Uncle Jack won't be back till Monday afternoon.

ALGERNON That is a great disappointment. I am obliged to go up by the first train on Monday morning. I have a business appointment that I am anxious ... to miss.

CECILY Couldn't you miss it anywhere but in London?

ALGERNON No: the appointment is in London.

CECILY Well, I know, of course, how important it is not to keep a business engagement, if one wants to retain any sense of the beauty of life, but still I think you had better wait till Uncle Jack arrives. I know he wants to speak to you about your emigrating.

ALGERNON About my what?

CECILY Your emigrating. He has gone up to buy your outfit.

ALGERNON I certainly wouldn't let Jack buy my outfit. He has no taste in neckties at all.

CECILY I don't think you will require neckties. Uncle Jack is sending you to Australia.

ALGERNON Australia! I'd sooner die.

CECILY Well, he said at dinner on Wednesday night, that you would have to choose between this world, the next world, and Australia.

ALGERNON Oh, well! The accounts I have received of Australia and the next world are not particularly encouraging. This world is good enough for me, cousin Cecily.

CECILY Yes, but are you good enough for it?

Algernon I'm afraid I'm not that. That is why I want you to reform me. You might make that your mission, if you don't mind, cousin Cecily.

Cecily I'm afraid I've no time, this afternoon.

Algernon Well, would you mind my reforming myself this afternoon?

Cecily It is rather Quixotic° of you. But I think you should try.

Algernon I will. I feel better already.

Cecily You are looking a little worse.

Algernon That is because I am hungry.

Cecily How thoughtless of me. I should have remembered that when one is going to lead an entirely new life, one requires regular and wholesome meals. Won't you come in?

Algernon Thank you. Might I have a buttonhole first? I have never any appetite unless I have a buttonhole first.

Cecily A Maréchal Niel?° (*Picks up scissors.*)

Algernon No, I'd sooner have a pink rose.

Cecily Why? (*Cuts a flower.*)

Algernon Because you are like a pink rose, cousin Cecily.

Cecily I don't think it can be right for you to talk to me like that. Miss Prism never says such things to me.

Algernon Then Miss Prism is a short-sighted old lady. (*Cecily puts the rose in his buttonhole.*) You are the prettiest girl I ever saw.

Cecily Miss Prism says that all good looks are a snare.

Algernon They are a snare that every sensible man would like to be caught in.

Cecily Oh, I don't think I would care to catch a sensible man. I shouldn't know what to talk to him about.

They pass into the house. Miss Prism and Dr Chasuble return.

MISS PRISM You are too much alone, dear Dr Chasuble. You should get married. A misanthrope I can understand – a womanthrope, never!

CHASUBLE (*With a scholar's shudder.*°) Believe me, I do not deserve so neologistic a phrase. The precept as well as the practice of the Primitive° Church was distinctly against matrimony.

MISS PRISM (*Sententiously.*) That is obviously the reason why the Primitive Church has not lasted up to the present day. And you do not seem to realise, dear Doctor, that by persistently remaining single, a man converts himself into a permanent public temptation. Men should be more careful; this very celibacy leads weaker vessels astray.

CHASUBLE But is a man not equally attractive when married?

MISS PRISM No married man is ever attractive except to his wife.

CHASUBLE And often, I've been told, not even to her.

MISS PRISM That depends on the intellectual sympathies of the woman. Maturity can always be depended on. Ripeness can be trusted. Young women are green. (*Dr Chasuble starts.*) I spoke horticulturally. My metaphor was drawn from fruit. But where is Cecily?

CHASUBLE Perhaps she followed us to the schools.

Enter Jack slowly from the back of the garden. He is dressed in the deepest mourning, with crape hatband and black gloves.

MISS PRISM Mr Worthing!

CHASUBLE Mr Worthing?

MISS PRISM This is indeed a surprise. We did not look for you till Monday afternoon.

Jack (*Shakes Miss Prism's hand in tragic manner.*) I have returned sooner than I expected. Dr Chasuble, I hope you are well?

Chasuble Dear Mr Worthing, I trust this garb of woe does not betoken some terrible calamity?

Jack My brother.

Miss Prism More shameful debts and extravagance?

Chasuble Still leading his life of pleasure?

Jack (*Shaking his head.*) Dead!

Chasuble Your brother Ernest dead?

Jack Quite dead.

Miss Prism What a lesson for him! I trust he will profit by it.

Chasuble Mr Worthing, I offer you my sincere condolence. You have at least the consolation of knowing that you are always the most generous and forgiving of brothers.

Jack Poor Ernest! He had many faults, but it is a sad, sad blow.

Chasuble Very sad indeed. Were you with him at the end?

Jack No. He died abroad; in Paris, in fact. I had a telegram last night from the manager of the Grand Hotel.

Chasuble Was the cause of death mentioned?

Jack A severe chill, it seems.

Miss Prism As a man sows, so shall he reap.

Chasuble (*Raising his hand.*) Charity, dear Miss Prism, charity! None of us are perfect. I myself am peculiarly susceptible to draughts. Will the interment take place here?

Jack No. He seems to have expressed a desire to be buried in Paris.

Chasuble In Paris! (*Shakes his head.*) I fear that hardly points to any very serious state of mind at the last.

You would no doubt wish me to make some slight allusion to this tragic domestic affliction next Sunday. (*Jack presses his hand convulsively.*) My sermon on the meaning of the manna° in the wilderness can be adapted to almost any occasion, joyful, or, as in the present case, distressing. (*All sigh.*) I have preached it at harvest celebrations, christenings, confirmations, on days of humiliation and festal days. The last time I delivered it was in the Cathedral, as a charity sermon on behalf of the Society for the Prevention of Discontent among the Upper Orders. The Bishop, who was present, was much struck by some of the analogies I drew.

JACK Ah! that reminds me, you mentioned christenings I think, Dr Chasuble? I suppose you know how to christen all right? (*Dr Chasuble looks astounded.*) I mean, of course, you are continually christening, aren't you?

MISS PRISM It is, I regret to say, one of the Rector's most constant duties in this parish. I have often spoken to the poorer classes on the subject. But they don't seem to know what thrift° is.

CHASUBLE But is there any particular infant in whom you are interested, Mr Worthing? Your brother was, I believe, unmarried, was he not?

JACK Oh yes.

MISS PRISM (*Bitterly.*) People who live entirely for pleasure usually are.

JACK But it is not for any child, dear Doctor. I am very fond of children. No! the fact is, I would like to be christened myself, this afternoon, if you have nothing better to do.

CHASUBLE But surely, Mr Worthing, you have been christened already?

JACK I don't remember anything about it.

CHASUBLE But have you any grave doubts on the subject?

JACK I certainly intend to have. Of course I don't know if the thing would bother you in any way, or if you think I am a little too old now.

CHASUBLE Not at all. The sprinkling, and, indeed, the immersion of adults is a perfectly canonical practice.

JACK Immersion!

CHASUBLE You need have no apprehensions. Sprinkling is all that is necessary, or indeed I think advisable. Our weather is so changeable. At what hour would you wish the ceremony performed?

JACK Oh, I might trot round about five if that would suit you.

CHASUBLE Perfectly, perfectly! In fact I have two similar ceremonies to perform at that time. A case of twins that occurred recently in one of the outlying cottages on your own estate. Poor Jenkins the carter, a most hard-working man.

JACK Oh! I don't see much fun in being christened along with other babies. It would be childish. Would half-past five do?

CHASUBLE Admirably! Admirably! (*Takes out watch.*) And now, dear Mr Worthing, I will not intrude any longer into a house of sorrow. I would merely beg you not to be too much bowed down by grief. What seem to us bitter trials are often blessings in disguise.

MISS PRISM This seems to me a blessing of an extremely obvious kind.

Enter Cecily from the house.

CECILY Uncle Jack! Oh, I am pleased to see you back. But what horrid clothes you have got on. Do go and change them.

MISS PRISM Cecily!

CHASUBLE My child! my child!
> *Cecily goes towards Jack; he kisses her brow in a melancholy manner.*

CECILY What is the matter, Uncle Jack? Do look happy! You look as if you had toothache, and I have got such a surprise for you. Who do you think is in the dining-room? Your brother!

JACK Who?

CECILY Your brother Ernest. He arrived about half an hour ago.

JACK What nonsense! I haven't got a brother.

CECILY Oh, don't say that. However badly he may have behaved to you in the past he is still your brother. You couldn't be so heartless as to disown him. I'll tell him to come out. And you will shake hands with him, won't you, Uncle Jack?
> *Runs back into the house.*

CHASUBLE These are very joyful tidings.

MISS PRISM After we had all been resigned to his loss, his sudden return seems to me peculiarly distressing.

JACK My brother is in the dining-room? I don't know what it all means. I think it is perfectly absurd.
> *Enter Algernon and Cecily hand in hand. They come slowly up to Jack.*

JACK Good heavens! (*Motions Algernon away.*)

ALGERNON Brother John, I have come down from town to tell you that I am very sorry for all the trouble I have given you, and that I intend to lead a better life in the future. (*Jack glares at him and does not take his hand.*)

CECILY Uncle Jack, you are not going to refuse your own brother's hand?

JACK Nothing will induce me to take his hand. I think his coming down here disgraceful. He knows perfectly well why.

CECILY Uncle Jack, do be nice. There is some good in every one. Ernest has just been telling me about his poor invalid friend Mr Bunbury whom he goes to visit so often. And surely there must be much good in one who is kind to an invalid, and leaves the pleasures of London to sit by a bed of pain.

JACK Oh! he has been talking about Bunbury, has he?

CECILY Yes, he has told me all about poor Mr Bunbury, and his terrible state of health.

JACK Bunbury! Well, I won't have him talk to you about Bunbury or about anything else. It is enough to drive one perfectly frantic.

ALGERNON Of course I admit that the faults were all on my side. But I must say that I think that Brother John's coldness to me is peculiarly painful. I expected a more enthusiastic welcome, especially considering it is the first time I have come here.

CECILY Uncle Jack, if you don't shake hands with Ernest I will never forgive you.

JACK Never forgive me?

CECILY Never, never, never!

JACK Well, this is the last time I shall ever do it. (*Shakes hands with Algernon and glares.*)

CHASUBLE It's pleasant, is it not, to see so perfect a reconciliation? I think we might leave the two brothers together.

MISS PRISM Cecily, you will come with us.

CECILY Certainly, Miss Prism. My little task of reconciliation is over.

CHASUBLE You have done a beautiful action to-day, dear child.

MISS PRISM We must not be premature in our judgments.

CECILY I feel very happy.

They all go off except Jack and Algernon.

JACK You young scoundrel, Algy, you must get out of this place as soon as possible. I don't allow any Bunburying here.

Enter Merriman.

MERRIMAN I have put Mr Ernest's things in the room next to yours, sir. I suppose that is all right?

JACK What?

MERRIMAN Mr Ernest's luggage, sir. I have unpacked it and put it in the room next to your own.

JACK His luggage?

MERRIMAN Yes, sir. Three portmanteaus, a dressing-case,° two hat-boxes, and a large luncheon-basket.

ALGERNON I am afraid I can't stay more than a week this time.

JACK Merriman, order the dog-cart° at once. Mr Ernest has been suddenly called back to town.

MERRIMAN Yes, sir.

Goes back into the house.

ALGERNON What a fearful liar you are, Jack. I have not been called back to town at all.

JACK Yes, you have.

ALGERNON I haven't heard anyone call me.

JACK Your duty as a gentleman calls you back.

ALGERNON My duty as a gentleman has never interfered with my pleasures in the smallest degree.

JACK I can quite understand that.

ALGERNON Well, Cecily is a darling.

JACK You are not to talk of Miss Cardew like that. I don't like it.

ALGERNON Well, I don't like your clothes. You look perfectly ridiculous in them. Why on earth don't you go up and change? It is perfectly childish to be in deep mourning for a man who is actually staying for a whole week with you in your house as a guest. I call it grotesque.

JACK You are certainly not staying with me for a whole week as a guest or anything else. You have got to leave … by the four-five train.

ALGERNON I certainly won't leave you so long as you are in mourning. It would be most unfriendly. If I were in mourning you would stay with me, I suppose. I should think it very unkind if you didn't.

JACK Well, will you go if I change my clothes?

ALGERNON Yes, if you are not too long. I never saw anybody take so long to dress, and with such little result.

JACK Well, at any rate, that is better than being always over-dressed as you are.

ALGERNON If I am occasionally a little over-dressed, I make up for it by being always immensely over-educated.

JACK Your vanity is ridiculous, your conduct an outrage, and your presence in my garden utterly absurd. However, you have got to catch the four-five, and I hope you will have a pleasant journey back to town. This Bunburying, as you call it, has not been a great success for you.

Goes into the house.

ALGERNON I think it has been a great success. I'm in love with Cecily, and that is everything.

Enter Cecily at the back of the garden. She picks up the can and begins to water the flowers.

But I must see her before I go, and make arrangements for another Bunbury. Ah, there she is.

CECILY Oh, I merely came back to water the roses. I thought you were with Uncle Jack.

ALGERNON He's gone to order the dog-cart for me.

CECILY Oh, is he going to take you for a nice drive?

ALGERNON He's going to send me away.

CECILY Then have we got to part?

ALGERNON I am afraid so. It's a very painful parting.

CECILY It is always painful to part from people whom one has known for a very brief space of time. The absence of old friends one can endure with equanimity. But even a momentary separation from anyone to whom one has just been introduced is almost unbearable.

ALGERNON Thank you.

Enter Merriman.

MERRIMAN The dog-cart is at the door, sir.

(*Algernon looks appealingly at Cecily.*)

CECILY It can wait, Merriman ... for ... five minutes.

MERRIMAN Yes, Miss.

Exit Merriman.

ALGERNON I hope, Cecily, I shall not offend you if I state quite frankly and openly that you seem to me to be in every way the visible personification of absolute perfection.

CECILY I think your frankness does you great credit, Ernest. If you will allow me, I will copy your remarks into my diary. (*Goes over to table and begins writing in diary.*)

ALGERNON Do you really keep a diary? I'd give anything to look at it. May I?

CECILY Oh no. (*Puts her hand over it.*) You see, it is simply a very young girl's record of her own thoughts and impressions, and consequently meant for publication. When it appears in volume form I hope you will order a copy. But pray, Ernest, don't stop. I delight in taking down from dictation. I have reached 'absolute perfection'. You can go on. I am quite ready for more.

ALGERNON (*Somewhat taken aback.*) Ahem! Ahem!

Cecily Oh, don't cough, Ernest. When one is dictating one should speak fluently and not cough. Besides, I don't know how to spell a cough. (*Writes as Algernon speaks.*)

Algernon (*Speaking very rapidly.*) Cecily, ever since I first looked upon your wonderful and incomparable beauty, I have dared to love you wildly, passionately, devotedly, hopelessly.

Cecily I don't think that you should tell me that you love me wildly, passionately, devotedly, hopelessly. Hopelessly doesn't seem to make much sense, does it?

Algernon Cecily!

Enter Merriman.

Merriman The dog-cart is waiting, sir.

Algernon Tell it to come round next week, at the same hour.

Merriman (*Looks at Cecily, who makes no sign.*) Yes, sir.

Merriman retires.

Cecily Uncle Jack would be very much annoyed if he knew you were staying on till next week, at the same hour.

Algernon Oh, I don't care about Jack. I don't care for anybody in the whole world but you. I love you, Cecily. You will marry me, won't you?

Cecily You silly boy! Of course. Why, we have been engaged for the last three months.

Algernon For the last three months?

Cecily Yes, it will be exactly three months on Thursday.

Algernon But how did we become engaged?

Cecily Well, ever since dear Uncle Jack first confessed to us that he had a younger brother who was very wicked and bad, you of course have formed the chief topic of conversation between myself and Miss Prism. And of course a man who is much talked about is always very attractive. One feels there must be something in him, after all. I daresay it was foolish of me, but I fell in love with you, Ernest.

ALGERNON Darling. And when was the engagement actually settled?

CECILY On the 14th of February last.* Worn out by your entire ignorance of my existence, I determined to end the matter one way or the other, and after a long struggle with myself I accepted you under this dear old tree here. The next day I bought this little ring in your name, and this is the little bangle with the true lover's knot I promised you always to wear.

ALGERNON Did I give you this? It's very pretty, isn't it?

CECILY Yes, you've wonderfully good taste, Ernest. It's the excuse I've always given for your leading such a bad life. And this is the box in which I keep all your dear letters. (*Kneels at table, opens box, and produces letters tied up with blue ribbon.*)

ALGERNON My letters! But, my own sweet Cecily, I have never written you any letters.

CECILY You need hardly remind me of that, Ernest. I remember only too well that I was forced to write your letters for you. I wrote always three times a week, and sometimes oftener.

ALGERNON Oh, do let me read them, Cecily?

CECILY Oh, I couldn't possibly. They would make you far too conceited. (*Replaces box.*) The three you wrote me after I had broken off the engagement are so beautiful, and so badly spelled, that even now I can hardly read them without crying a little.

ALGERNON But was our engagement ever broken off?

CECILY Of course it was. On the 22nd of last March. You can see the entry if you like. (*Shows diary.*)

'To-day I broke off engagement with Ernest. I feel it is better to do so. The weather still continues charming.'

ALGERNON But why on earth did you break it off? What had I done? I had done nothing at all. Cecily, I am very much hurt indeed to hear you broke it off. Particularly when the weather was so charming.

CECILY It would hardly have been a really serious engagement if it hadn't been broken off at least once. But I forgave you before the week was out.

ALGERNON (*Crossing to her, and kneeling.*) What a perfect angel you are, Cecily.

CECILY You dear romantic boy. (*He kisses her, she puts her fingers through his hair.*) I hope your hair curls naturally, does it?

ALGERNON Yes, darling, with a little help from others.

CECILY I am so glad.

ALGERNON You'll never break off our engagement again, Cecily?

CECILY I don't think I could break it off now that I have actually met you. Besides, of course, there is the question of your name.

ALGERNON Yes, of course. (*Nervously.*)

CECILY You must not laugh at me, darling, but it had always been a girlish dream of mine to love some one whose name was Ernest. (*Algernon rises.*) There is something in that name that seems to inspire absolute confidence. I pity any poor married woman whose husband is not called Ernest.

ALGERNON But, my dear child, do you mean to say you could not love me if I had some other name?

CECILY But what name?

ALGERNON Oh, any name you like – Algernon – for instance ...

CECILY But I don't like the name of Algernon.

ALGERNON Well, my own dear, sweet, loving little darling, I really can't see why you should object to the name of Algernon. It is not at all a bad name. In fact, it is rather an aristocratic name. Half of the chaps who get into the Bankruptcy Court are called Algernon. But seriously, Cecily ... (*Moving to her.*) ... if my name was Algy, couldn't you love me?

CECILY (*Rising.*) I might respect you, Ernest, I might admire your character, but I fear that I should not be able to give you my undivided attention.

ALGERNON Ahem! Cecily! (*Picking up hat.*) Your Rector here is, I suppose, thoroughly experienced in the practice of all the rites and ceremonials of the Church?

CECILY Oh, yes. Dr Chasuble is a most learned man. He has never written a single book, so you can imagine how much he knows.

ALGERNON I must see him at once on a most important christening – I mean on most important business.

CECILY Oh!

ALGERNON I shan't be away more than half an hour.

CECILY Considering that we have been engaged since February the 14th, and that I only met you to-day for the first time, I think it is rather hard that you should leave me for so long a period as half an hour. Couldn't you make it twenty minutes?

ALGERNON I'll be back in no time.

Kisses her and rushes down the garden.

CECILY What an impetuous boy he is! I like his hair so much. I must enter his proposal in my diary.

Enter Merriman.

MERRIMAN A Miss Fairfax has just called to see Mr Worthing. On very important business, Miss Fairfax states.

CECILY Isn't Mr Worthing in his library?

Merriman Mr Worthing went over in the direction of the Rectory some time ago.

Cecily Pray ask the lady to come out here; Mr Worthing is sure to be back soon. And you can bring tea.

Merriman Yes, Miss.

Goes out.

Cecily Miss Fairfax! I suppose one of the many good elderly women who are associated with Uncle Jack in some of his philanthropic work in London. I don't quite like women who are interested in philanthropic work. I think it is so forward of them.

Enter Merriman.

Merriman Miss Fairfax.

Enter Gwendolen. Exit Merriman.

Cecily (*Advancing to meet her.*) Pray let me introduce myself to you. My name is Cecily Cardew.

Gwendolen Cecily Cardew? (*Moving to her and shaking hands.*) What a very sweet name! Something tells me that we are going to be great friends. I like you already more than I can say. My first impressions of people are never wrong.

Cecily How nice of you to like me so much after we have known each other such a comparatively short time. Pray sit down.

Gwendolen (*Still standing up.*) I may call you Cecily, may I not?

Cecily With pleasure!

Gwendolen And you will always call me Gwendolen, won't you?

Cecily If you wish.

Gwendolen Then that is all quite settled, is it not?

Cecily I hope so.

A pause. They both sit down together.

GWENDOLEN Perhaps this might be a favourable opportunity for my mentioning who I am. My father is Lord Bracknell. You have never heard of papa, I suppose?

CECILY I don't think so.

GWENDOLEN Outside the family circle, papa, I am glad to say, is entirely unknown. I think that is quite as it should be. The home seems to me to be the proper sphere for the man. And certainly once a man begins to neglect his domestic duties he becomes painfully effeminate, does he not? And I don't like that. It makes men so very attractive. Cecily, mamma, whose views on education are remarkably strict, has brought me up to be extremely short-sighted; it is part of her system; so do you mind my looking at you through my glasses?

CECILY Oh! not at all, Gwendolen. I am very fond of being looked at.

GWENDOLEN (*After examining Cecily carefully through a lorgnette.*) You are here on a short visit, I suppose.

CECILY Oh no! I live here.

GWENDOLEN (*Severely.*) Really? Your mother, no doubt, or some female relative of advanced years, resides here also?

CECILY Oh no! I have no mother, nor, in fact, any relations.

GWENDOLEN Indeed?

CECILY My dear guardian, with the assistance of Miss Prism, has the arduous task of looking after me.

GWENDOLEN Your guardian?

CECILY Yes, I am Mr Worthing's ward.

GWENDOLEN Oh! It is strange he never mentioned to me that he had a ward. How secretive of him! He grows more interesting hourly. I am not sure, however, that the news inspires me with feelings of unmixed delight. (*Rising and going to her.*) I am very fond of you, Cecily; I have liked you ever since I met you! But I am bound to state that now that I know that you are Mr Worthing's ward, I cannot help expressing a wish you were – well, just a little older than you seem to be – and not quite so very alluring in appearance. In fact, if I may speak candidly –

CECILY Pray do! I think that whenever one has anything unpleasant to say, one should always be quite candid.

GWENDOLEN Well, to speak with perfect candour, Cecily, I wish that you were fully forty-two, and more than usually plain for your age. Ernest has a strong upright nature. He is the very soul of truth and honour. Disloyalty would be as impossible to him as deception. But even men of the noblest possible moral character are extremely susceptible to the influence of the physical charms of others. Modern, no less than Ancient History, supplies us with many most painful examples of what I refer to. If it were not so, indeed, History would be quite unreadable.

CECILY I beg your pardon, Gwendolen, did you say Ernest?

GWENDOLEN Yes.

CECILY Oh, but it is not Mr Ernest Worthing who is my guardian. It is his brother – his elder brother.

GWENDOLEN (*Sitting down again.*) Ernest never mentioned to me that he had a brother.

CECILY I am sorry to say they have not been on good terms for a long time.

GWENDOLEN Ah! that accounts for it. And now that I think of it, I have never heard any man mention his brother. The subject seems distasteful to most men. Cecily, you have lifted a load from my mind. I was growing almost anxious. It would have been terrible if any cloud had come across a friendship like ours, would it not? Of course you are quite, quite sure that it is not Mr Ernest Worthing who is your guardian?

CECILY Quite sure. (*A pause.*) In fact, I am going to be his.

GWENDOLEN (*Inquiringly.*) I beg your pardon?

CECILY (*Rather shy and confidingly.*) Dearest Gwendolen, there is no reason why I should make a secret of it to you. Our little county newspaper is sure to chronicle the fact next week. Mr Ernest Worthing and I are engaged to be married.

GWENDOLEN (*Quite politely, rising.*) My darling Cecily, I think there must be some slight error. Mr Ernest Worthing is engaged to me. The announcement will appear in the *Morning Post* on Saturday at the latest.

CECILY (*Very politely, rising.*) I am afraid you must be under some misconception. Ernest proposed to me exactly ten minutes ago. (*Shows diary.*)

GWENDOLEN (*Examines diary through her lorgnette carefully.*) It is certainly very curious, for he asked me to be his wife yesterday afternoon at 5.30. If you would care to verify the incident, pray do so. (*Produces diary of her own.*) I never travel without my diary. One should always have something sensational to read in the train. I am so sorry, dear Cecily, if it is any disappointment to you, but I am afraid I have the prior claim.

CECILY It would distress me more than I can tell you, dear Gwendolen, if it caused you any mental or physical anguish, but I feel bound to point out that since Ernest proposed to you he clearly has changed his mind.

GWENDOLEN (*Meditatively.*) If the poor fellow has been entrapped into any foolish promise I shall consider it my duty to rescue him at once, and with a firm hand.

CECILY (*Thoughtfully and sadly.*) Whatever unfortunate entanglement my dear boy may have got into, I will never reproach him with it after we are married.

GWENDOLEN Do you allude to me, Miss Cardew, as an entanglement? You are presumptuous. On an occasion of this kind it becomes more than a moral duty to speak one's mind. It becomes a pleasure.

CECILY Do you suggest, Miss Fairfax, that I entrapped Ernest into an engagement? How dare you? This is no time for wearing the shallow mask of manners. When I see a spade I call it a spade.

GWENDOLEN (*Satirically.*) I am glad to say that I have never seen a spade. It is obvious that our social spheres have been widely different.

Enter Merriman, followed by the footman. He carries a salver, table cloth, and plate stand. Cecily is about to retort. The presence of the servants exercises a restraining influence, under which both girls chafe.

MERRIMAN Shall I lay tea here as usual, Miss?

CECILY (*Sternly, in a calm voice.*) Yes, as usual.

Merriman begins to clear table and lay cloth. A long pause. Cecily and Gwendolen glare at each other.

GWENDOLEN Are there many interesting walks in the vicinity, Miss Cardew?

CECILY Oh! yes! a great many. From the top of one of the hills quite close one can see five counties.

GWENDOLEN Five counties! I don't think I should like that; I hate crowds.

CECILY (*Sweetly.*) I suppose that is why you live in town?

Gwendolen bites her lip, and beats her foot nervously with her parasol.

GWENDOLEN (*Looking round.*) Quite a well-kept garden this is, Miss Cardew.

CECILY So glad you like it, Miss Fairfax.

GWENDOLEN I had no idea there were any flowers in the country.

CECILY Oh, flowers are as common here, Miss Fairfax, as people are in London.

GWENDOLEN Personally I cannot understand how anybody manages to exist in the country, if anybody who is anybody does. The country always bores me to death.

CECILY Ah! This is what the newspapers call agricultural depression, is it not? I believe the aristocracy are suffering very much from it just at present. It is almost an epidemic amongst them, I have been told. May I offer you some tea, Miss Fairfax?

GWENDOLEN (*With elaborate politeness.*) Thank you. (*Aside.*) Detestable girl! But I require tea!

CECILY (*Sweetly.*) Sugar?

GWENDOLEN (*Superciliously.*) No, thank you. Sugar is not fashionable any more. (*Cecily looks angrily at her, takes up the tongs and puts four lumps of sugar into the cup.*)

CECILY (*Severely.*) Cake or bread and butter?

GWENDOLEN (*In a bored manner.*) Bread and butter, please. Cake is rarely seen at the best houses nowadays.

CECILY (*Cuts a very large slice of cake and puts it on the tray.*) Hand that to Miss Fairfax.

Merriman does so, and goes out with footman. Gwendolen drinks the tea and makes a grimace. Puts down cup at once, reaches out her hand to the bread and butter, looks at it, and finds it is cake. Rises in indignation.

GWENDOLEN You have filled my tea with lumps of sugar, and though I asked most distinctly for bread and butter, you have given me cake. I am known for the gentleness of my disposition, and the extraordinary sweetness of my nature, but I warn you, Miss Cardew, you may go too far.

CECILY (*Rising.*) To save my poor, innocent, trusting boy from the machinations of any other girl there are no lengths to which I would not go.

GWENDOLEN From the moment I saw you I distrusted you. I felt that you were false and deceitful. I am never deceived in such matters. My first impressions of people are invariably right.

CECILY It seems to me, Miss Fairfax, that I am trespassing on your valuable time. No doubt you have many other calls of a similar character to make in the neighbourhood.

Enter Jack.

GWENDOLEN (*Catching sight of him.*) Ernest! My own Ernest!

JACK Gwendolen! Darling! (*Offers to kiss her.*)

GWENDOLEN (*Drawing back.*) A moment! May I ask if you are engaged to be married to this young lady? (*Points to Cecily.*)

JACK (*Laughing.*) To dear little Cecily! Of course not! What could have put such an idea into your pretty little head?

GWENDOLEN Thank you. You may! (*Offers her cheek.*)

CECILY (*Very sweetly.*) I knew there must be some misunderstanding, Miss Fairfax. The gentleman whose arm is at present round your waist is my guardian, Mr John Worthing.

GWENDOLEN I beg your pardon?

CECILY This is Uncle Jack.

GWENDOLEN (*Receding.*) Jack! Oh!
   Enter Algernon.

CECILY Here is Ernest.

ALGERNON (*Goes straight over to Cecily without noticing anyone else.*) My own love! (*Offers to kiss her.*)

CECILY (*Drawing back.*) A moment, Ernest! May I ask you – are you engaged to be married to this young lady?

ALGERNON (*Looking round.*) To what young lady? Good heavens! Gwendolen!

CECILY Yes! to good heavens, Gwendolen, I mean to Gwendolen.

ALGERNON (*Laughing.*) Of course not! What could have put such an idea into your pretty little head?

CECILY Thank you. (*Presenting her cheek to be kissed.*) You may. (*Algernon kisses her.*)

GWENDOLEN I felt there was some slight error, Miss Cardew. The gentleman who is now embracing you is my cousin, Mr Algernon Moncrieff.

CECILY (*Breaking away from Algernon.*) Algernon Moncrieff! Oh! (*The two girls move towards each other and put their arms round each other's waists as if for protection.*)

CECILY Are you called Algernon?

ALGERNON I cannot deny it.

CECILY Oh!

GWENDOLEN Is your name really John?

JACK (*Standing rather proudly.*) I could deny it if I liked. I could deny anything if I liked. But my name certainly is John. It has been John for years.

CECILY (*To Gwendolen.*) A gross deception has been practised on both of us.

GWENDOLEN My poor wounded Cecily!

CECILY My sweet wronged Gwendolen!

GWENDOLEN (*Slowly and seriously.*) You will call me sister, will you not?

> *They embrace. Jack and Algernon groan and walk up and down.*

CECILY (*Rather brightly.*) There is just one question I would like to be allowed to ask my guardian.

GWENDOLEN An admirable idea! Mr Worthing, there is just one question I would like to be permitted to put to you. Where is your brother Ernest? We are both engaged to be married to your brother Ernest, so it is a matter of some importance to us to know where your brother Ernest is at present.

JACK (*Slowly and hesitatingly.*) Gwendolen – Cecily – it is very painful for me to be forced to speak the truth. It is the first time in my life that I have ever been reduced to such a painful position, and I am really quite inexperienced in doing anything of the kind. However, I will tell you quite frankly that I have no brother Ernest. I have no brother at all. I never had a brother in my life and I certainly have not the smallest intention of ever having one in the future.

CECILY (*Surprised.*) No brother at all?

JACK (*Cheerily.*) None!

GWENDOLEN (*Severely.*) Had you never a brother of any kind?

JACK (*Pleasantly.*) Never. Not even of any kind.

GWENDOLEN I am afraid it is quite clear, Cecily, that neither of us is engaged to be married to anyone.

CECILY It is not a very pleasant position for a young girl suddenly to find herself in. Is it?

GWENDOLEN Let us go into the house. They will hardly venture to come after us there.

CECILY No, men are so cowardly, aren't they?

> *They retire into the house with scornful looks.*

JACK This ghastly state of things is what you call Bunburying, I suppose?

ALGERNON Yes, and a perfectly wonderful Bunbury it is. The most wonderful Bunbury I have ever had in my life.

JACK Well, you've no right whatsoever to Bunbury here.

ALGERNON That is absurd. One has a right to Bunbury anywhere one chooses. Every serious Bunburyist knows that.

JACK Serious Bunburyist! Good heavens!

ALGERNON Well, one must be serious about something, if one wants to have any amusement in life. I happen to be serious about Bunburying. What on earth you are serious about I haven't got the remotest idea. About everything, I should fancy. You have such an absolutely trivial nature.

JACK Well, the only small satisfaction I have in the whole of this wretched business is that your friend Bunbury is quite exploded. You won't be able to run down to the country quite so often as you used to do, dear Algy. And a very good thing too.

ALGERNON Your brother is a little off colour, isn't he, dear Jack? You won't be able to disappear to London quite so frequently as your wicked custom was. And not a bad thing either.

JACK As for your conduct towards Miss Cardew, I must say that your taking in a sweet, simple, innocent girl like that is quite inexcusable. To say nothing of the fact that she is my ward.

ALGERNON I can see no possible defence at all for your deceiving a brilliant, clever, thoroughly experienced young lady like Miss Fairfax. To say nothing of the fact that she is my cousin.

JACK I wanted to be engaged to Gwendolen, that is all. I love her.

ALGERNON Well, I simply wanted to be engaged to
Cecily. I adore her.

JACK There is certainly no chance of your marrying
Miss Cardew.

ALGERNON I don't think there is much likelihood, Jack,
of you and Miss Fairfax being united.

JACK Well, that is no business of yours.

ALGERNON If it was my business, I wouldn't talk about
it. (*Begins to eat muffins.*) It is very vulgar to talk
about one's business. Only people like stockbrokers
do that, and then merely at dinner parties.

JACK How you can sit there, calmly eating muffins
when we are in this horrible trouble, I can't make
out. You seem to me to be perfectly heartless.

ALGERNON Well, I can't eat muffins in an agitated
manner. The butter would probably get on my cuffs.
One should always eat muffins quite calmly. It is the
only way to eat them.

JACK I say it's perfectly heartless your eating muffins at
all, under the circumstances.

ALGERNON When I am in trouble, eating is the only thing
that consoles me. Indeed, when I am in really great
trouble, as anyone who knows me intimately will
tell you, I refuse everything except food and drink.
At the present moment I am eating muffins because
I am unhappy. Besides, I am particularly fond of
muffins. (*Rising.*)

JACK (*Rising.*) Well, there is no reason why you should
eat them all in that greedy way. (*Takes muffins from
Algernon.*)

ALGERNON (*Offering tea-cake.*) I wish you would have
tea-cake instead. I don't like tea-cake.

JACK Good heavens! I suppose a man may eat his own
muffins in his own garden.

ALGERNON But you have just said it was perfectly heartless to eat muffins.

JACK I said it was perfectly heartless of you, under the circumstances. That is a very different thing.

ALGERNON That may be. But the muffins are the same. (*He seizes the muffin-dish from Jack.*)

JACK Algy, I wish to goodness you would go.

ALGERNON You can't possibly ask me to go without having some dinner. It's absurd. I never go without my dinner. No one ever does, except vegetarians and people like that. Besides I have just made arrangements with Dr Chasuble to be christened at a quarter to six under the name of Ernest.

JACK My dear fellow, the sooner you give up that nonsense the better. I made arrangements this morning with Dr Chasuble to be christened myself at 5.30, and I naturally will take the name of Ernest. Gwendolen would wish it. We cannot both be christened Ernest. It's absurd. Besides, I have a perfect right to be christened if I like. There is no evidence at all that I have ever been christened by anybody. I should think it extremely probable I never was, and so does Dr Chasuble. It is entirely different in your case. You have been christened already.

ALGERNON Yes, but I have not been christened for years.

JACK Yes, but you have been christened. That is the important thing.

ALGERNON Quite so. So I know my constitution can stand it. If you are not quite sure about your ever having been christened, I must say I think it rather dangerous your venturing on it now. It might make you very unwell. You can hardly have forgotten that some one very closely connected with you was very nearly carried off this week in Paris by a severe chill.

JACK Yes, but you said yourself that a severe chill was not hereditary.

ALGERNON It usen't to be, I know – but I daresay it is now. Science is always making wonderful improvements in things.

JACK (*Picking up the muffin-dish.*) Oh, that is nonsense; you are always talking nonsense.

ALGERNON Jack, you are at the muffins again! I wish you wouldn't. There are only two left. (*Takes them.*) I told you I was particularly fond of muffins.

JACK But I hate tea-cake.

ALGERNON Why on earth then do you allow tea-cake to be served up for your guests? What ideas you have of hospitality!

JACK Algernon! I have already told you to go. I don't want you here. Why don't you go!

ALGERNON I haven't quite finished my tea yet! and there is still one muffin left.

Jack groans, and sinks into a chair. Algernon still continues eating.

ACT DROP

Third Act

*Scene: Morning-room at the Manor House. Gwendolen and
Cecily are at the window, looking out into the garden.*

GWENDOLEN The fact that they did not follow us at once
into the house, as any one else would have done,
seems to me to show that they have some sense of
shame left.

CECILY They have been eating muffins. That looks like
repentance.

GWENDOLEN (*After a pause.*) They don't seem to notice
us at all. Couldn't you cough?

CECILY But I haven't got a cough.

GWENDOLEN They're looking at us. What effrontery!

CECILY They're approaching. That's very forward of
them.

GWENDOLEN Let us preserve a dignified silence.

CECILY Certainly. It's the only thing to do now.
*Enter Jack followed by Algernon. They whistle some
dreadful popular air from a British Opera.*

GWENDOLEN This dignified silence seems to produce an
unpleasant effect.

CECILY A most distasteful one.

GWENDOLEN But we will not be the first to speak.

CECILY Certainly not.

GWENDOLEN Mr Worthing, I have something very
particular to ask you. Much depends on your reply.

CECILY Gwendolen, your common sense is invaluable.
Mr Moncrieff, kindly answer me the following
question. Why did you pretend to be my guardian's
brother?

ALGERNON In order that I might have an opportunity of meeting you.

CECILY (*To Gwendolen.*) That certainly seems a satisfactory explanation, does it not?

GWENDOLEN Yes, dear, if you can believe him.

CECILY I don't. But that does not affect the wonderful beauty of his answer.

GWENDOLEN True. In matters of grave importance, style, not sincerity, is the vital thing. Mr Worthing, what explanation can you offer to me for pretending to have a brother? Was it in order that you might have an opportunity of coming up to town to see me as often as possible?

JACK Can you doubt it, Miss Fairfax?

GWENDOLEN I have the gravest doubts upon the subject. But I intend to crush them. This is not the moment for German scepticism.◊ (*Moving to Cecily.*) Their explanations appear to be quite satisfactory, especially Mr Worthing's. That seems to me to have the stamp of truth upon it.

CECILY I am more than content with what Mr Moncrieff said. His voice alone inspires one with absolute credulity.

GWENDOLEN Then you think we should forgive them?

CECILY Yes. I mean no.

GWENDOLEN True! I had forgotten. There are principles at stake that one cannot surrender. Which of us should tell them? The task is not a pleasant one.

CECILY Could we not both speak at the same time?

GWENDOLEN An excellent idea! I nearly always speak at the same time as other people. Will you take the time from me?

CECILY Certainly. (*Gwendolen beats time with uplifted finger.*)

GWENDOLEN and CECILY (*Speaking together.*) Your Christian names are still an insuperable barrier. That is all!

JACK and ALGERNON (*Speaking together.*) Our Christian names! Is that all? But we are going to be christened this afternoon.

GWENDOLEN (*To Jack.*) For my sake you are prepared to do this terrible thing?

JACK I am.

CECILY (*To Algernon.*) To please me you are ready to face this fearful ordeal?

ALGERNON I am!

GWENDOLEN How absurd to talk of the equality of the sexes! Where questions of self-sacrifice are concerned, men are infinitely beyond us.

JACK We are. (*Clasps hands with Algernon.*)

CECILY They have moments of physical courage of which we women know absolutely nothing.

GWENDOLEN (*To Jack.*) Darling!

ALGERNON (*To Cecily.*) Darling! (*They fall into each other's arms.*)

> *Enter Merriman. When he enters he coughs loudly, seeing the situation.*

MERRIMAN Ahem! Ahem! Lady Bracknell!

JACK Good heavens!

> *Enter Lady Bracknell. The couples separate in alarm. Exit Merriman.*

LADY BRACKNELL Gwendolen! What does this mean?

GWENDOLEN Merely that I am engaged to be married to Mr Worthing, mamma.

LADY BRACKNELL Come here. Sit down. Sit down immediately. Hesitation of any kind is a sign of mental decay in the young, of physical weakness in the old. (*Turns to Jack.*) Apprised, sir, of my daughter's sudden flight by her trusty maid, whose confidence I purchased by means of a small coin, I followed her at once by a luggage train.° Her unhappy father is, I am glad to say, under the impression that she is attending a more than usually lengthy lecture by the University Extension Scheme on the Influence of a permanent income on Thought. I do not propose to undeceive him. Indeed I have never undeceived him on any question. I would consider it wrong. But of course, you will clearly understand that all communication between yourself and my daughter must cease immediately from this moment. On this point, as indeed on all points, I am firm.

JACK I am engaged to be married to Gwendolen, Lady Bracknell!

LADY BRACKNELL You are nothing of the kind, sir. And now as regards Algernon! ... Algernon!

ALGERNON Yes, Aunt Augusta.

LADY BRACKNELL May I ask if it is in this house that your invalid friend Mr Bunbury resides?

ALGERNON (*Stammering.*) Oh! No! Bunbury doesn't live here. Bunbury is somewhere else at present. In fact, Bunbury is dead.

LADY BRACKNELL Dead! When did Mr Bunbury die? His death must have been extremely sudden.

ALGERNON (*Airily.*) Oh! I killed Bunbury this afternoon. I mean poor Bunbury died this afternoon.

LADY BRACKNELL What did he die of?

ALGERNON Bunbury? Oh, he was quite exploded.

LADY BRACKNELL Exploded! Was he the victim of a revolutionary outrage? I was not aware that Mr Bunbury was interested in social legislation. If so, he is well punished for his morbidity.

ALGERNON My dear Aunt Augusta, I mean he was found out! The doctors found out that Bunbury could not live, that is what I mean – so Bunbury died.

LADY BRACKNELL   He seems to have had great confidence in the opinion of his physicians. I am glad, however, that he made up his mind at the last to some definite course of action, and acted under proper medical advice. And now that we have finally got rid of this Mr Bunbury, may I ask, Mr Worthing, who is that young person whose hand my nephew Algernon is now holding in what seems to me a peculiarly unnecessary manner?

JACK   That lady is Miss Cecily Cardew, my ward. (*Lady Bracknell bows coldly to Cecily.*)

ALGERNON   I am engaged to be married to Cecily, Aunt Augusta.

LADY BRACKNELL   I beg your pardon?

CECILY   Mr Moncrieff and I are engaged to be married, Lady Bracknell.

LADY BRACKNELL   (*With a shiver, crossing to the sofa and sitting down.*) I do not know whether there is anything peculiarly exciting in the air of this particular part of Hertfordshire, but the number of engagements that go on seems to me considerably above the proper average that statistics have laid down for our guidance. I think some preliminary inquiry on my part would not be out of place. Mr Worthing, is Miss Cardew at all connected with any of the larger railway stations in London? I merely desire information. Until yesterday I had no idea that there were any families or persons whose origin was a Terminus. (*Jack looks perfectly furious, but restrains himself.*)

JACK   (*In a clear, cold voice.*) Miss Cardew is the grand-daughter of the late Mr Thomas Cardew of 149 Belgrave Square, S.W.; Gervase Park, Dorking, Surrey; and the Sporran, Fifeshire, N.B.$^\diamond$

LADY BRACKNELL That sounds not unsatisfactory. Three addresses always inspire confidence, even in tradesmen. But what proof have I of their authenticity?

JACK I have carefully preserved the Court Guides of the period. They are open to your inspection, Lady Bracknell.

LADY BRACKNELL (*Grimly.*) I have known strange errors in that publication.

JACK Miss Cardew's family solicitors are Messrs Markby, Markby, and Markby.

LADY BRACKNELL Markby, Markby, and Markby? A firm of the very highest position in their profession. Indeed I am told that one of the Mr Markbys is occasionally to be seen at dinner parties. So far I am satisfied.

JACK (*Very irritably.*) How extremely kind of you, Lady Bracknell! I have also in my possession, you will be pleased to hear, certificates of Miss Cardew's birth, baptism, whooping cough, registration, vaccination, confirmation, and the measles; both the German and the English variety.

LADY BRACKNELL Ah! A life crowded with incident, I see; though perhaps somewhat too exciting for a young girl. I am not myself in favour of premature experiences. (*Rises, looks at her watch.*) Gwendolen! the time approaches for our departure. We have not a moment to lose. As a matter of form, Mr Worthing, I had better ask you if Miss Cardew has any little fortune?

JACK Oh! about a hundred and thirty thousand pounds in the Funds.° That is all. Goodbye, Lady Bracknell. So pleased to have seen you.

LADY BRACKNELL (*Sitting down again.*) A moment, Mr Worthing. A hundred and thirty thousand pounds!

And in the Funds! Miss Cardew seems to me a most attractive young lady, now that I look at her. Few girls of the present day have any really solid qualities, any of the qualities that last, and improve with time. We live, I regret to say, in an age of surfaces. (*To Cecily.*) Come over here, dear. (*Cecily goes across.*) Pretty child! your dress is sadly simple, and your hair seems almost as Nature might have left it. But we can soon alter all that. A thoroughly experienced French maid produces a really marvellous result in a very brief space of time. I remember recommending one to young Lady Lancing, and after three months her own husband did not know her.

JACK   And after six months nobody knew her.

LADY BRACKNELL   (*Glares at Jack for a few moments. Then bends, with a practised smile, to Cecily.*) Kindly turn round, sweet child. (*Cecily turns completely round.*) No, the side view is what I want. (*Cecily presents her profile.*) Yes, quite as I expected. There are distinct social possibilities in your profile. The two weak points in our age are its want of principle and its want of profile. The chin a little higher, dear. Style largely depends on the way the chin is worn. They are worn very high, just at present. Algernon!

ALGERNON   Yes, Aunt Augusta!

LADY BRACKNELL   There are distinct social possibilities in Miss Cardew's profile.

ALGERNON   Cecily is the sweetest, dearest, prettiest girl in the whole world. And I don't care twopence about social possibilities.

LADY BRACKNELL   Never speak disrespectfully of Society, Algernon. Only people who can't get into it do that. (*To Cecily.*) Dear child, of course you know that Algernon has nothing but his debts to depend upon.

But I do not approve of mercenary marriages. When I married Lord Bracknell I had no fortune of any kind. But I never dreamed for a moment of allowing that to stand in my way. Well, I suppose I must give my consent.

Algernon Thank you, Aunt Augusta.

Lady Bracknell Cecily, you may kiss me!

Cecily (*Kisses her.*) Thank you, Lady Bracknell.

Lady Bracknell You may also address me as Aunt Augusta for the future.

Cecily Thank you, Aunt Augusta.

Lady Bracknell The marriage, I think, had better take place quite soon.

Algernon Thank you, Aunt Augusta.

Cecily Thank you, Aunt Augusta.

Lady Bracknell To speak frankly, I am not in favour of long engagements. They give people the opportunity of finding out each other's character before marriage, which I think is never advisable.

Jack I beg your pardon for interrupting you, Lady Bracknell, but this engagement is quite out of the question. I am Miss Cardew's guardian, and she cannot marry without my consent until she comes of age. That consent I absolutely decline to give.

Lady Bracknell Upon what grounds, may I ask? Algernon is an extremely, I may almost say an ostentatiously, eligible young man. He has nothing, but he looks everything. What more can one desire?

Jack It pains me very much to have to speak frankly to you, Lady Bracknell, about your nephew, but the fact is that I do not approve at all of his moral character. I suspect him of being untruthful.

(*Algernon and Cecily look at him in indignant amazement.*)

LADY BRACKNELL   Untruthful! My nephew Algernon?
Impossible! He is an Oxonian. ⬦

JACK   I fear there can be no possible doubt about the
matter. This afternoon during my temporary
absence in London on an important question of
romance, he obtained admission to my house by
means of the false pretence of being my brother.
Under an assumed name he drank, I've just been
informed by my butler, an entire pint bottle of my
Perrier-Jouet, Brut, '89; ⬦ a wine I was specially
reserving for myself. Continuing his disgraceful
deception, he succeeded in the course of the
afternoon in alienating the affections of my only
ward. He subsequently stayed to tea, and devoured
every single muffin. And what makes his conduct all
the more heartless is, that he was perfectly well
aware from the first that I have no brother, that I
never had a brother, and that I don't intend to have
a brother, not even of any kind. I distinctly told him
so myself yesterday afternoon.

LADY BRACKNELL   Ahem! Mr Worthing, after careful
consideration I have decided entirely to overlook my
nephew's conduct to you.

JACK   That is very generous of you, Lady Bracknell. My
own decision, however, is unalterable. I decline to
give my consent.

LADY BRACKNELL   (*To Cecily.*) Come here, sweet child.
(*Cecily goes over.*) How old are you, dear?

CECILY   Well, I am really only eighteen, but I always
admit to twenty when I go to evening parties.

LADY BRACKNELL   You are perfectly right in making some
slight alteration. Indeed, no woman should ever be
quite accurate about her age. It looks so calculating.
... (*In a meditative manner.*) Eighteen, but admitting
to twenty at evening parties. Well, it will not be very

long before you are of age and free from the restraints of tutelage. So I don't think your guardian's consent is, after all, a matter of any importance.

JACK Pray excuse me, Lady Bracknell, for interrupting you again, but it is only fair to tell you that according to the terms of her grandfather's will Miss Cardew does not come legally of age till she is thirty-five.

LADY BRACKNELL That does not seem to me to be a grave objection. Thirty-five is a very attractive age. London society is full of women of the very highest birth who have, of their own free choice, remained thirty-five for years. Lady Dumbleton is an instance in point. To my own knowledge she has been thirty-five ever since she arrived at the age of forty, which was many years ago now. I see no reason why our dear Cecily should not be even still more attractive at the age you mention than she is at present. There will be a large accumulation of property.

CECILY Algy, could you wait for me till I was thirty-five?

ALGERNON Of course I could, Cecily. You know I could.

CECILY Yes, I felt it instinctively, but I couldn't wait all that time. I hate waiting even five minutes for anybody. It always makes me rather cross. I am not punctual myself, I know, but I do like punctuality in others, and waiting, even to be married, is quite out of the question.

ALGERNON Then what is to be done, Cecily?

CECILY I don't know, Mr Moncrieff.

LADY BRACKNELL My dear Mr Worthing, as Miss Cardew states positively that she cannot wait till she is thirty-five – a remark which I am bound to say

seems to me to show a somewhat impatient nature –
I would beg of you to reconsider your decision.

JACK But my dear Lady Bracknell, the matter is entirely
in your own hands. The moment you consent to my
marriage with Gwendolen, I will most gladly allow
your nephew to form an alliance with my ward.

LADY BRACKNELL (*Rising and drawing herself up.*) You
must be quite aware that what you propose is out of
the question.

JACK Then a passionate celibacy is all that any of us
can look forward to.

LADY BRACKNELL That is not the destiny I propose for
Gwendolen. Algernon, of course, can choose for
himself. (*Pulls out her watch.*) Come, dear,
(*Gwendolen rises*) we have already missed five, if
not six, trains. To miss any more might expose us to
comment on the platform.

    Enter Dr Chasuble.

CHASUBLE Everything is quite ready for the christenings.

LADY BRACKNELL The christenings, sir! Is not that
somewhat premature?

CHASUBLE (*Looking rather puzzled, and pointing to Jack
and Algernon.*) Both these gentlemen have expressed
a desire for immediate baptism.

LADY BRACKNELL At their age? The idea is grotesque and
irreligious! Algernon, I forbid you to be baptised. I
will not hear of such excesses. Lord Bracknell would
be highly displeased if he learned that that was the
way in which you wasted your time and money.

CHASUBLE Am I to understand then that there are to be
no christenings at all this afternoon?

JACK I don't think that, as things are now, it would be
of much practical value to either of us, Dr Chasuble.

CHASUBLE I am grieved to hear such sentiments from
you, Mr Worthing. They savour of the heretical

views of the Anabaptists,* views that I have completely refuted in four of my unpublished sermons. However, as your present mood seems to be one peculiarly secular, I will return to the church at once. Indeed, I have just been informed by the pew-opener that for the last hour and a half Miss Prism has been waiting for me in the vestry.

LADY BRACKNELL (*Starting.*) Miss Prism! Did I hear you mention a Miss Prism?

CHASUBLE Yes, Lady Bracknell. I am on my way to join her.

LADY BRACKNELL Pray allow me to detain you for a moment. This matter may prove to be one of vital importance to Lord Bracknell and myself. Is this Miss Prism a female of repellent aspect, remotely connected with education?

CHASUBLE (*Somewhat indignantly.*) She is the most cultivated of ladies, and the very picture of respectability.

LADY BRACKNELL It is obviously the same person. May I ask what position she holds in your household?

CHASUBLE (*Severely.*) I am a celibate, madam.

JACK (*Interposing.*) Miss Prism, Lady Bracknell, has been for the last three years Miss Cardew's esteemed governess and valued companion.

LADY BRACKNELL In spite of what I hear of her, I must see her at once. Let her be sent for.

CHASUBLE (*Looking off.*) She approaches; she is nigh.
Enter Miss Prism hurriedly.

MISS PRISM I was told you expected me in the vestry dear Canon. I have been waiting for you there for an hour and three-quarters. (*Catches sight of Lady Bracknell, who has fixed her with a stony glare. Miss Prism grows pale and quails. She looks anxiously round as if desirous to escape.*)

LADY BRACKNELL (*In a severe, judicial voice.*) Prism! (*Miss Prism bows her head in shame.*) Come here, Prism! (*Miss Prism approaches in a humble manner.*) Prism! Where is that baby? (*General consternation. The Canon starts back in horror, Algernon and Jack pretend to be anxious to shield Cecily and Gwendolen from hearing the details of a terrible public scandal.*) Twenty-eight years ago, Prism, you left Lord Bracknell's house, Number 104, Upper Grosvenor Square, in charge of a perambulator that contained a baby of the male sex. You never returned. A few weeks later, through the elaborate investigations of the Metropolitan police, the perambulator was discovered at midnight standing by itself in a remote corner of Bayswater. It contained the manuscript of a three-volume novel of more than usually revolting sentimentality. (*Miss Prism starts in involuntary indignation.*) But the baby was not there. (*Everyone looks at Miss Prism.*) Prism! Where is that baby?

   A pause.

MISS PRISM Lady Bracknell, I admit with shame that I do not know. I only wish I did. The plain facts of the case are these. On the morning of the day you mention, a day that is for ever branded on my memory, I prepared as usual to take the baby out in its perambulator. I had also with me a somewhat old, but capacious hand-bag in which I had intended to place the manuscript of a work of fiction that I had written during my few unoccupied hours. In a moment of mental abstraction, for which I can never forgive myself, I deposited the manuscript in the bassinet,° and placed the baby in the hand-bag.

JACK (*Who had been listening attentively.*) But where did you deposit the hand-bag?

MISS PRISM   Do not ask me, Mr Worthing.

JACK   Miss Prism, this is a matter of no small
importance to me. I insist on knowing where you
deposited the hand-bag that contained that infant.

MISS PRISM   I left it in the cloak-room of one of the
larger railway stations in London.

JACK   What railway station?

MISS PRISM   (*Quite crushed.*) Victoria. The Brighton
line. (*Sinks into a chair.*)

JACK   I must retire to my room for a moment.
Gwendolen, wait here for me.

GWENDOLEN   If you are not too long, I will wait here for
you all my life.

    Exit Jack in great excitement.

CHASUBLE   What do you think this means, Lady
Bracknell?

LADY BRACKNELL   I dare not even suspect, Dr Chasuble. I
need hardly tell you that in families of high position
strange coincidences are not supposed to occur.
They are hardly considered the thing.

    *Noises heard overhead as if some one was throwing
trunks about. Everyone looks up.*

CECILY   Uncle Jack seems strangely agitated.

CHASUBLE   Your guardian has a very emotional nature.

LADY BRACKNELL   This noise is extremely unpleasant. It
sounds as if he was having an argument. I dislike
arguments of any kind. They are always vulgar, and
often convincing.

CHASUBLE   (*Looking up.*) It has stopped now. (*The noise
is redoubled.*)

LADY BRACKNELL   I wish he would arrive at some
conclusion.

GWENDOLEN   This suspense is terrible. I hope it will last.

    *Enter Jack with a hand-bag of black leather in his
hand.*

Jack (*Rushing over to Miss Prism.*) Is this the hand-bag, Miss Prism? Examine it carefully before you speak. The happiness of more than one life depends on your answer.

Miss Prism (*Calmly.*) It seems to be mine. Yes, here is the injury it received through the upsetting of a Gower Street◇ omnibus in younger and happier days. Here is the stain on the lining caused by the explosion of a temperance beverage, an incident that occurred at Leamington.◇ And here, on the lock, are my initials. I had forgotten that in an extravagant mood I had had them placed there. The bag is undoubtedly mine. I am delighted to have it so unexpectedly restored to me. It has been a great inconvenience being without it all these years.

Jack (*In a pathetic voice.*) Miss Prism, more is restored to you than this hand-bag. I was the baby you placed in it.

Miss Prism (*Amazed.*) You?

Jack (*Embracing her.*) Yes – mother!

Miss Prism (*Recoiling in indignant astonishment.*) Mr Worthing. I am unmarried!

Jack Unmarried! I do not deny that is a serious blow. But after all, who has the right to cast a stone◇ against one who has suffered? Cannot repentance wipe out an act of folly? Why should there be one law for men, and another for women? Mother, I forgive you. (*Tries to embrace her again.*)

Miss Prism (*Still more indignant.*) Mr Worthing, there is some error. (*Pointing to Lady Bracknell.*) There is the lady who can tell you who you really are.

Jack (*After a pause.*) Lady Bracknell, I hate to seem inquisitive, but could you kindly inform me who I am?

LADY BRACKNELL I am afraid that the news I have to give you will not altogether please you. You are the son of my poor sister, Mrs Moncrieff, and consequently Algernon's elder brother.

JACK Algy's elder brother! Then I have a brother after all. I knew I had a brother! I always said I had a brother! Cecily – how could you have ever doubted that I had a brother? (*Seizes hold of Algernon.*) Dr Chasuble, my unfortunate brother. Miss Prism, my unfortunate brother. Gwendolen, my unfortunate brother. Algy, you young scoundrel, you will have to treat me with more respect in the future. You have never behaved to me like a brother in all your life.

ALGERNON Well, not till to-day, old boy, I admit. I did my best, however, though I was out of practice.
Shakes hands.

GWENDOLEN (*To Jack.*) My own! But what own are you? What is your Christian name, now that you have become some one else?

JACK Good heavens! … I had quite forgotten that point. Your decision on the subject of my name is irrevocable, I suppose?

GWENDOLEN I never change, except in my affections.

CECILY What a noble nature you have, Gwendolen!

JACK Then the question had better be cleared up at once. Aunt Augusta, a moment. At the time when Miss Prism left me in the hand-bag, had I been christened already?

LADY BRACKNELL Every luxury that money could buy, including christening, had been lavished on you by your fond and doting parents.

JACK Then I was christened! That is settled. Now, what name was I given? Let me know the worst.

LADY BRACKNELL Being the eldest son you were naturally christened after your father.

JACK (*Irritably.*) Yes, but what was my father's Christian name?

LADY BRACKNELL (*Meditatively.*) I cannot at the present moment recall what the General's Christian name was. But I have no doubt he had one. He was eccentric, I admit. But only in later years. And that was the result of the Indian climate, and marriage, and indigestion, and other things of that kind.

JACK Algy! Can't you recollect what our father's Christian name was?

ALGERNON My dear boy, we were never even on speaking terms. He died before I was a year old.

JACK His name would appear in the Army Lists of the period, I suppose, Aunt Augusta?

LADY BRACKNELL The General was essentially a man of peace, except in his domestic life. But I have no doubt his name would appear in any military directory.

JACK The Army Lists of the last forty years are here. These delightful records should have been my constant study. (*Rushes to bookcase and tears the books out.*) M. Generals ... Mallam, Maxbohm, Magley, what ghastly names they have – Markby, Migsby, Mobbs, Moncrieff! Lieutenant 1840, Captain, Lieutenant-Colonel, Colonel, General 1869, Christian names, Ernest John. (*Puts book very quietly down and speaks quite calmly.*) I always told you, Gwendolen, my name was Ernest, didn't I? Well, it is Ernest after all. I mean it naturally is Ernest.

LADY BRACKNELL Yes, I remember now that the General was called Ernest. I knew I had some particular reason for disliking the name.

GWENDOLEN   Ernest! My own Ernest! I felt from the first that you could have no other name!

JACK   Gwendolen, it is a terrible thing for a man to find out suddenly that all his life he has been speaking nothing but the truth. Can you forgive me?

GWENDOLEN   I can. For I feel that you are sure to change.

JACK   My own one!

CHASUBLE   (*To Miss Prism.*) Laetitia! (*Embraces her.*)

MISS PRISM   (*Enthusiastically.*) Frederick! At last!

ALGERNON   Cecily! (*Embraces her.*) At last!

JACK   Gwendolen! (*Embraces her.*) At last!

LADY BRACKNELL   My nephew, you seem to be displaying signs of triviality.

JACK   On the contrary, Aunt Augusta, I've now realised for the first time in my life the vital Importance of Being Earnest.

TABLEAU

CURTAIN

Resource Notes

RESOURCE NOTES

Who has written *The Importance of Being Earnest* and why?

Glittering prizes

Oscar Fingal O'Flahertie Wills Wilde was born in Dublin on 16 October 1854. His parents were Sir William Wilde, a distinguished, if eccentric, eye surgeon, and Lady Jane Wilde, a poet and fervent advocate for Ireland's freedom from English rule. Even though his parents were unconventional, Wilde's education was thoroughly typical for a member of the Anglo-Irish (i.e. non-Catholic) establishment: Portora Royal School, the 'Protestant' university Trinity College Dublin, and then Oxford. He had a brilliant academic career at both Dublin and Oxford, winning many scholarships and prizes, including the prestigious Newdigate prize for poetry in 1878. When he settled in London in 1879 he aimed to win the biggest prize, to be famous in the capital of the world's leading nation.

A collection of poems was published in 1881 and two plays, *Vera or the Nihilists* and *The Duchess of Padua*, were produced, but with little success. If Wilde was initially unsuccessful as a writer he made an immediate impact as a personality. At Oxford he had been deeply influenced by two writers, Walter Pater and John Ruskin, who, with differing emphases, advocated beliefs that were labelled Aestheticism – the celebration of beauty and art as the highest purpose in life. Wilde became so conspicuous an apostle for 'art for art's sake' that when the composers W. S. Gilbert and Arthur Sullivan lampooned Aestheticism in their operetta *Patience* (1881), the central character, Bunthorne, was recognisably modelled on him. A successful lecture tour of America in 1882, to publicise the operetta, confirmed Wilde's reputation as a dazzling talker who seemed able to charm and outrage simultaneously.

By 1887 Wilde was married with two sons and needed more money. He was editor of the magazine *Women's World* for two years but, more significantly, he became a professional writer, producing a wide range of stories, essays, articles, a novel (*The Picture of Dorian Gray*), and the plays that brought him, if only briefly, a fortune to embellish his fame.

Outsider and outcast

As an Irishman, albeit a well-educated Protestant with a private income, Wilde was by birth an outsider in English society. As chief populariser and publicist of the Aesthetic movement he flaunted views that were unconventional, indeed oppositional, in the world of late Victorian England. Beyond art, his sympathies with socialist politics further distanced him from conventional thinking. But such flamboyant disregard for convention, rather than obstructing his acceptance, gave him a role; he became a kind of court jester, with a licence to shock. At the first night of *Lady Windermere's Fan* (1892), responding to calls for the author, Wilde appeared on stage wearing mauve gloves, a blue carnation and smoking a cigarette (in the presence of ladies!) to compliment the audience on its intelligent response:

> 'I congratulate you on the great success of your
> performance, which persuades me that you think
> almost as highly of the play as I do myself.'

If the egotism (and the cigarette smoking) shocked a few people, they were outnumbered by those who revelled in his audacity.

But while he was gaining fame through proclaiming his scorn for conventional behaviour, Wilde was also hiding a guilty secret – his homosexual relationships. Although his marriage appears to have been a happy one, Wilde had a series of attachments to young, beautiful men, culminating in an intense affair with Lord Alfred Douglas, son of the Marquess of Queensberry, a notoriously irascible bully. Homosexual practices were a criminal offence. Queensberry's suspicions about his son and Wilde led him to leave a card at Wilde's club on which he wrote, with an aristocratic disregard for correct spelling, 'To Oscar Wilde posing Somdomite'. Urged on by Douglas, who loathed his father, Wilde sued for criminal libel, lost the case and his own subsequent trial led to imprisonment, ruin, exile and death.

✦ *Activity*

Paradox (in the sense of 'statement contrary to received opinion') is a major source of humour in the play. From Algernon's perverse view of who establishes standards in Victorian society – 'if the lower orders don't set us a good example, what on earth is the use of them?' – to Jack's shameful confession that he has spent his whole life 'speaking nothing but the truth' the play is full of them.

a Re-read a short section of the play and note how often common-sense views are inverted.

b Are the paradoxes simply comic? Richard Ellmann, Wilde's most recent biographer, claimed that 'Wilde was conducting ... an anatomy of his society, and a radical reconsideration of its ethics' (*Oscar Wilde*, p. xiv; see Further Reading).

How do you think paradoxes would make an audience reconsider its values?

Victorian values

The Shorter Oxford English Dictionary defines 'earnest' as 'of persons: Serious; usually in emphatic sense, intensely serious, in purpose, feeling, conviction, or action; sincerely zealous'.

Seriousness and sincerity were two foundation stones of Victorian values. Hard work and a sense of duty were also significant virtues. The great Victorian advocate of self-improvement, Samuel Smiles (1812–1904), whose most famous book, *Self-Help* (1859), was one of the biggest best-sellers of the nineteenth century, argues their importance, not simply for the individual but also for the nation:

> 'As steady application to work is the healthiest
> training for every individual, so is it the best
> discipline of a state. Honourable industry travels the
> same road with duty; and providence has closely
> linked both with happiness.'

Such virtues might gain the admiration of the former British Prime Minister Margaret Thatcher, but in Oscar Wilde they excited merely contempt.

In 'De Profundis', his long letter to his lover Lord Alfred Douglas, written while in prison, Wilde catalogued the defects of the dominant middle-class culture of his age:

> '... their heavy inaccessibility to ideas, their dull
> respectability, their tedious orthodoxy, their
> worship of vulgar success, their entire
> preoccupation with the gross materialistic side of
> life, and their ridiculous estimate of themselves and
> their importance ...'

The three plays that precede *The Importance of Being Earnest* (*Lady Windermere's Fan*, *A Woman of No Importance* and *An Ideal Husband*) are more overtly satirical than this play. They also involve aristocratic characters, settings with which the affluent audiences could immediately identify themselves, and characters speaking Wildean dialogue. But they are written as melodrama, rather than farce (these terms are further discussed in the next section) and they dramatise social comments on late Victorian society, such as moral hypocrisy or the position of women.

✦ *Activities*

1 Wilde believed that the 'work of art is always unique'. It would be useful to read one of the earlier plays to see how, in relation to Wilde's other plays at least, *The Importance of Being Earnest* is unique.

a Choose one of the three social comment plays to read and discuss with other students.

b Present your views on the similarities and differences between this play and *The Importance of Being Earnest*. Is *Earnest* unusual?

2 Throughout the play all the characters make very confident statements about what is right and wrong. Re-read Act 1.

a Note all the words that are associated with approval / disapproval.

b What subjects provoke such moral comments? List them in two columns – 'serious' and 'trivial'.

c What do you think is the effect of characters speaking with equal sincerity and conviction about both serious and trivial topics?

✦

Date	The main events of Oscar Wilde's life
1854	Oscar Wilde born in Dublin.
1864–71	Attends Portora Royal School, Enniskillen.
1871–74	Attends Trinity College Dublin.
1874–78	Attends Magdalen College, Oxford.
1880	*Vera or the Nihilists* printed privately.
1881	Gilbert and Sullivan's *Patience* – central character Bunthorne associated with Wilde.
1882	Lecture tour of USA and Canada.
1884	Marries Constance Lloyd.
1885	First son, Cyril, is born.
1886	Second son, Vyvyan, is born.
1887	Editor of *Women's World*.
1890	*The Picture of Dorian Gray* published.
1891	Meets Lord Alfred Douglas, friend and lover.
1892	*Lady Windermere's Fan* performed.
1893	*A Woman of No Importance* performed.
1895 3 Jan 14 Feb 5 April 25 May	*An Ideal Husband* performed. *The Importance of Being Earnest* performed. Marquess of Queensberry acquitted of libel; Wilde is arrested. Wilde convicted of indecency and sentenced to two years' imprisonment with hard labour.
1896	Death of Wilde's mother.
1897	Wilde released from prison; goes to Europe.
1898	*The Ballad of Reading Gaol* published.
1899	*The Importance of Being Earnest* published.
1900	Wilde dies in Paris.

What type of text is *The Importance of Being Earnest*?

This play refers to a number of serious topics: class and money; snobbery and the decline of the aristocracy; love and marriage. It includes subjects that are potentially painful: deceit, death, the loss of a baby. Most of these topics are incidental, but some are integral to the plot. However, to say that the play is *about* any of these large, sombre issues would seem misleading because *The Importance of Being Earnest* is, first and finally, a comedy.

If it was a really unconventional text, an audience could not laugh at it because it would not be understood. What makes the play ingenious is that a number of different kinds of comedy, kinds that are familiar to audiences – such as farce, satire, visual and verbal humour – are combined into a single, coherent whole.

◆ *Activities*

1   Select a few current television comedy programmes. Are serious, possibly distressing, issues touched on in these programmes? If so, in what ways are they handled?

2   Categorise some television comedy programmes using a chart with headings such as 'physical/visual', 'farce', 'satire', 'verbal humour'. Add other headings of your own.

Farce

If Wilde's previous three plays were melodramas, it might seem odd that he should suddenly produce a farce, but the difference between the two genres is not that great. Both use similar ingredients: disguised identities, guilty secrets, revelation of the true facts. In melodrama the writer aims for pathos and in farce, humour. In both genres the plot moves forward at a swift pace, especially towards the end. In both, a key source of the audience's enjoyment is that it knows more about what is going on than many characters do, but it is as surprised as they are by the climactic burst of revelations.

✦ *Activities*

1 Both farce and melodrama are currently unfashionable. Can you think of any recent films or television programmes that have elements of farce or melodrama?

2 List the key moments in the play where the audience has more knowledge than some (or all) of the characters on stage.

3 The plot moves forward quickly in this play, but the speeches have to be spoken quite slowly. Try reading a few pages at a fast pace.

a What is it about the language that makes such fast speaking so difficult?

b What is lost through such an accelerated pace?

4 Read again the final pages of the play, from Lady Bracknell's recognition of Miss Prism to the end. Aim to act this section in a melodramatic style, using the exaggerated gestures/movements, over-emphatic facial expressions and highly emotional speaking voice that are associated with melodrama.

Which speeches can sustain such a style and which seem unsuited to melodramatic acting?

Visual

The appearance of Jack in Act 2, 'dressed in the deepest mourning, with crape hatband and black gloves', is considered to be the visual highlight of the play. The characteristic responses of Chasuble and Miss Prism enhance the comedy of farcical confusion, but the audience will probably be laughing before a word is spoken. Why might this be?

Elsewhere in the play, examples of visual humour would depend on how actors respond to each other. A rather frenetic style of acting has become associated with British farce, with people rushing in and out of doors, lots of double-takes and bits of clothing, especially trousers, getting mislaid. Such a style would not suit the stateliness of Wilde's dialogue. The characters always speak with some seriousness, aristocratically unaware of any farcical chaos that may ensue. The British actor John Gielgud said:

> '"The Importance of Being Earnest" has to be played very strictly; it is like chamber music. You must not indulge yourself or caricature. You must play it with your tongue in your cheek like a solemn charade.'
> (Quoted by Michael Billington in 'A Personal Essay' in the Longman Study Text edition)

✦ *Activity*

Wilde offers some guidance in his stage directions, but they are not very detailed or prescriptive, therefore much of the 'business' on stage depends on the actors' (and director's) interpretation. Read again the scene in Act 2 when Gwendolen and Cecily take tea and 'glare at each other'. In pairs, act the scene a few times, each time aiming to make the antagonism more intense, through both the dialogue and physical movement.

How much emotion can be displayed before it becomes inappropriate to this play?

Satire

One of the first-night reviews of the play said that 'Mr Wilde makes his personages ridiculous, but ... he does not ridicule them.' Whatever their faults, Wilde seems to delight in his characters, rather than despise them.

Ridicule is a strong feature in classic satirical texts, such as Jonathan Swift's *Gulliver's Travels* (1726) or George Orwell's *Animal Farm* (1945). Other constituent features of satire are:
- a tone of anger, loathing, contempt;
- use of caricature, rather than characters, to make the portrayal of folly more emphatic through exaggeration;
- moral condemnation, usually with a clear sense of alternative, better ways of behaving;
- relating the society satirised to specific, contemporary problems in the writer's own time;
- criticisms of real people (e.g. Stalin as the ruthless Napoleon in *Animal Farm*).

✦ *Activities*

1   In Lady Bracknell, Miss Prism and Canon Chasuble, Wilde has been seen as satirising the aristocracy, education and the Church.

   What characteristics of these 'pillars of the establishment' are portrayed as ridiculous through these caricatures?

2   Lady Bracknell has been seen as an insensitive, bullying snob who threatens to thwart the romances of both Gwendolen/Jack and Cecily/Algernon. But, is she ever really hateful?

   What changes would you make in the portrayal of Lady Bracknell to turn her into a character whom the audience is meant to hate?

3   Is it significant that *all* the characters are ridiculous? Consider how your judgement of characters would be affected if there was some commentary from a character who was not ridiculous.

   Imagine you are either Lane or Merriman. Write diary entries that cover appropriate sections of the play. Express fully the amused contempt you have for your betters.

Verbal humour

Comedy can include a wide range of different kinds of verbal humour, from jokes, through word-play/puns to wit. If you look up 'wit' in the *Oxford English Dictionary* you will notice that it used to mean intellect, having the capacity to think and reason; indeed, William Shakespeare used it in that sense. By the time of Oscar Wilde it had narrowed to its current association with verbal expression:

> 'That quality of speech or writing which consists in the apt association of thought and expression, calculated to surprise and delight by its unexpectedness; later always with ref to the utterance of brilliant sparkling things in an amusing way.'

The witty dialogue is *the* characteristic of this play, the main source of its humour. What are its constituent features?

Dialogue

It is possible to have a witty monologue, but there are only a few brief moments in this play when a character is alone on stage. (Soliloquy, ever since Shakespeare, has been a key dramatic device for exploring a character's inner thoughts and feelings. Consider why you think Wilde never uses such a device in this play.) From the first conversation between Algernon and Lane, the play is dominated by repartee; the characters compete with one another to produce witty, smart replies to whatever is said. All the characters are involved, even the ridiculous stereotypes like Lady Bracknell, Miss Prism or Canon Chasuble, who might be expected to be merely victims of such humour.

✦ *Activity*

a Is any one character more witty than the others?

b Is there anyone who invariably wins the speaking competitions?

Epigram

An epigrammatic style is one which is pointed, concise, frequently antithetical (contrasting ideas). The connection with paradoxes (see page 95) is clear. In drama, such a style depends on relatively simple syntax and diction. Colon and semi-colon constructions are rare; complex sentences are infrequent; and the diction is not often elaborate.

✦ *Activity*

a Why is Lady Bracknell able to speak occasionally in long sentences?

b When Cecily and Gwendolen are briefly rivals for Ernest, their diction becomes more elaborate: 'Do you allude to me, Miss Cardew, as an entanglement?' Why might this be?

c The relatively simple language highlights the more pompous, pretentious utterances of Miss Prism and Canon Chasuble. Note examples of their more elaborate diction.

Interrogation

As part of the competition between characters, there is frequent use of a question–answer technique in the dialogue. There are moments of formal interrogation, such as Algernon's questioning of Jack about the cigarette case, Lady Bracknell's detailed examination of Mr Worthing's credentials or her 'judicial' assault on Miss Prism, but these are simply the more elaborate examples of a technique that underpins much of the play.

✦ *Activity*

In the examples above, one person is clearly in charge of the interrogation. Look at other examples in the play. Is that imbalance of power always present?

Further activities

1 One way to understand a text is to imitate it. Choose a situation and people you are familiar with (e.g. lunchtime in a student common room) and, in groups, improvise a dialogue involving the normal topics of conversation but expressed in a Wildean style.

a Does one character begin to dominate?

b Why do all the characters have to be assertive?

2 Wilde wrote some essays in dialogue form, most notably 'The Decay of Lying' and 'The Critic as Artist' (see Further Reading on page 123). They are written in the same paradoxical, epigrammatical style as this play, but both syntax and diction are much more elaborate. Read one of them.

a Why is such elaboration of language present in the essay but not in the play?

b What would you need to add to a section of dialogue from the essay to make it dramatic?

———————————————— ✦ ————————————————

How was *The Importance of Being Earnest* produced?

Before a word is spoken, it is clear that the play is located in an affluent sphere of society; the room is 'luxuriously and artistically furnished', a piano is being played and a servant is 'arranging afternoon tea'. The rest of the play amply confirms that initial impression: the characters are educated, rich people, most of whom do not work; the action moves from a luxurious 'bachelor's establishment' to a country house; the text is full of references to places, interests, habits, prejudices and aspirations familiar to a British middle/upper-class audience of the 1890s.

The London theatre of Wilde's time seems to have been divided into two contrasting audiences. The fashionable theatre-goers went to be seen and to be amused at those theatres dominated by actor-managers: St James's (George Alexander), Her Majesty's (Beerbohm Tree), Lyceum (Henry Irving). They enjoyed the predictable pleasures of lavishly staged Shakespeare, melodrama and farce. An audience that was more seriously interested in drama as an art form was drawn to the Independent Theatre Club (J.T. Grein), where they could watch the more unsettlingly radical plays of Henrik Ibsen (1828–1906) and George Bernard Shaw (1856–1950). However, despite the differing expectations of these two audiences, they formed a single, homogeneous one in that they were largely middle/upper-class people. Wilde's audience recognised themselves in his characters, how they spoke and dressed, in the furnishings of the rooms and, most importantly, in the assumptions about appropriate behaviour with which Wilde could create such comic mayhem.

✦ *Activities*

1 Research the clothes of middle/upper-class men and women in 1890s London and design costumes for some of the characters.

a How differently dressed would Lady Bracknell be from Cecily and Gwendolen?

b Would you want Algernon/Jack and Cecily/Gwendolen to be very different in appearance?

2 Research the interior decoration of late Victorian homes.
   What would be the differences between the two morning rooms – Algernon's flat and the Manor House?

3 Imagine you are the stage manager for a production of the play. Make an inventory of the props and furniture needed in each act.

4 Choose some current television soap operas and situation comedies. Make notes using the following headings:
   • class of main characters
   • clothing
   • speech styles
   • décor of interiors
   • main locations for meetings.

a What social classes are most frequently represented in these kinds of television programmes?

b Would you consider any programme to be a modern-day equivalent of *The Importance of Being Earnest*?

✦

How does *The Importance of Being Earnest* present its subject?

> 'In matters of grave importance, style, not sincerity,
> is the vital thing.'

Who says that? Algernon? Jack? Gwendolen? Cecily? The answer is Gwendolen, but it could have been any of them because all the main characters speak in the same style. They all speak like Oscar Wilde. The great Irish poet W.B. Yeats (1865–1939) was astonished when he first met Wilde because he had 'never before heard a man talking with perfect sentences'. He also said that:

> 'the dinner table was Wilde's event and made him
> the greatest talker of his time, and his plays and
> dialogues have what merit they possess from being
> now an imitation, now a record, of his talk.'
>
> (Ellman, p. 15)

Wilde's contemporary audience would immediately recognise themselves in the characters when the curtain rose. What the audience would not recognise in themselves, of course, is the ability of all the characters, even the servants, to be witty. In *De Profundis* (published in 1905), Wilde claimed that he:

> 'took the drama, the most objective form known to
> art, and made it as personal a mode of expression as
> the lyric or the sonnet.'

In those short forms a poet expresses thoughts and feelings directly to the reader; in drama, meanings are generally expressed through characters who are different from each other and, it is usually assumed, different from the writer.

Characters or caricatures?

If the four central characters of the play are simply vehicles for Wilde's own *bon mots*, then that contradicts the usual assumptions about dramatised characters. In responding to realist drama the audience is encouraged to believe that the characters are autonomous: they are differentiated from each other by subtle, or obvious, characteristics in their speech patterns; their personalities are made distinct through their differing responses to each other and the play's events; past histories can be imagined that have helped to form the characters in action on the stage; and, perhaps most crucially, they develop in significantly different ways during the course of the play.

Caricatures may well be quite starkly different from each other. What they say and how they say it will be characteristic and their response to events will be so distinct as to be predictable. But, they will not have the other two elements of autonomy: they will not have a history that can be imagined and they will not develop during the play.

◆ *Activities*

1 Hot-seating (responding to questions in the role of a character from the text) is a useful technique for exploring your views of a character. In small groups, try this technique by 'hot-seating' each of the four main characters in turn.

a How many specific facts do you have on which to base your interpretation of the character?

b How easy or difficult is it to invent details about your past life or your views on issues not dealt with in the play?

2 Choose a short speech that does not contain clues to the speaker's identity (e.g. names mentioned). Read the speech aloud to a partner. Can s/he tell who is speaking?

3 'Thought tracking' or inner voices: choose a short section of dialogue between two characters. In a group of four, rehearse a presentation in which two people read the dialogue while the other two speak the characters' inner thoughts and feelings which accompany the dialogue.

Identity

In Wilde's three social comedies, in his dialogue essays and in his novel *The Picture of Dorian Gray* (1890), there is one character who is witty, cynical, infatuated with style and ostentatiously unconventional about values. This figure of the dandy is the mouthpiece for Wilde in these other texts. In this play there are four dandies, two of whom are women; in the earlier plays the dandy is an isolated figure. The audience may delight in his witticisms but they are also able to reflect critically about him because he can be seen in relation to other characters who are not witty and cynical.

'Sincerity' or 'integrity' are not valid terms to describe a dandy. What matters instead is the glamour of the personality projected, the impact of the pose struck. If caricature suggests a very static sense of character then, in contrast, becoming a dandy suggests the possibility of change.

✦ *Activities*

1 The invention of characters is central to the play's plot, signalled at the beginning by Jack's invented brother and Algernon's invalid friend Bunbury.

   What other examples are there of characters creating themselves and their images of others?

2 Except for Cecily's and Gwendolen's eccentric attachment to the name Ernest, the attitude to love and courtship of all the major characters is highly conventional.

a What conventions of romance are observed, indeed insisted upon, in the play? Who does the insisting?

b Can you find any hint of sincere emotion or sexual attraction?

Fantasy

George Bernard Shaw, in his review of the play, objected to the 'scene between the two girls in the second act', which he thought was an imitation of a Gilbert and Sullivan operetta and that the 'unfortunate moment of Gilbertism breaks our belief in the humanity of the play' (in Beckson, pp. 194–195). He means not the scene when the girls are taking tea, but when they are rejoined by Jack and Algernon; the speeches become highly artificial, with frequent repetition of diction and syntax, accompanied by highly stylised movements between the characters. This artificiality is intensified at the beginning of Act 3, prior to the reappearance of Lady Bracknell, when the couples' speeches merge into single voices and their movements appear almost choreographed.

If these scenes 'break our belief in the humanity of the play', it is because they direct our attention to its theatricality; the characters speak like automata and any attempt at realism is discarded. Yet, the dream-like mood that this creates seems to exist mostly for a theatrical effect – the impact of the real world's reappearance in the formidable shape of Lady Bracknell. In comparison to these scenes, much of the rest of the play seems more realistic; but, despite the actual London addresses, the minute attention to upper-class rituals, especially its meals, how real is any of the play?

✦ *Activities*

1   'The characters know they are in a play, and they
     know what kind of play it is.'
                    (Richard Foster, 1956, in Tydeman, p. 165)

What examples can you find of a character self-consciously playing a role?

2 Rehearse the movements and speech in the scene between the couples at the beginning of Act 3.

How balletic can the movements be made before they become too absurd?

3 In most productions of the play, the actors speak in an upper-middle-class accent called Received Pronunciation. Choose any scene, one featuring Lady Bracknell would work particularly well, and read the dialogue in another accent: regional English (Yorkshire, Liverpool, North-East), Irish, American, Australian, Afro-Caribbean.

How possible is it to fit Wilde's syntax to the rhythm of such accents?

◆

Who reads/watches *The Importance of Being Earnest*? How do they interpret it?

Wilde said of the play that 'it is quite nonsensical and has no serious interest'. William Archer (1856–1924) wrote in his review of its first performance:

> 'What can a poor critic do with a play which raises no principle, whether of art or morals, creates its own canons and conventions and is nothing but an absolutely wilful expression of an irrepressibly witty personality? ... *The Importance of Being Earnest* ... imitates nothing, represents nothing, means nothing, is nothing ...'
>
> (1895, in Tydeman, p. 66)

The play questions the usual criteria for evaluating imaginative texts, especially drama. Such criteria rely on ideas of representation.

> 'Our vocabulary of approval for the drama is dominated by representational considerations like "truth to character", "truth to situation", or else by didactic ones like "social or moral vision". A dramatist who offers neither character nor social or moral vision would seem to be offering only triviality.'
>
> (Ian Gregor, 1966, in Tydeman, p. 125)

Perhaps because the play avoids such conventional interpretation it has attracted a wide range of divergent readings. Thinking about some of these views, testing your opinions against them, will extend your understanding of this 'Trivial Comedy for Serious People'.

'Clever as it was, it was his first really heartless play.'

(G.B. Shaw, 1930, in Ellmann, p. 95)

'Humanitarian considerations are out of place here; they belong to the middle class. Insensibility is the comic "vice" of the characters; it is also their charm and badge of prestige. Selfishness and servility are the moral alternatives presented ... Algernon Moncrieff and Cecily Cardew are, taken by themselves, unendurable; the meeching Dr. Chasuble, however, justifies their way of life by affording a comparison – it is better to be cruel than craven.'

(Mary McCarthy, 1947, in Ellmann, p. 109)

'Wilde depicts a world in which the socially endorsed certainties are continually evaporating; values respecting social class, education, the Church, money, love and the family undergo constant metamorphosis.'

(David Parker, 1974, in Tydeman, p. 172)

'... instead of presenting the problems of modern society directly, he flits around them, teasing them, declining to grapple with them. His wit is no searchlight into the darkness of modern life. It is a flickering, a coruscation, intermittently revealing the upper class of England in a harsh bizarre light.'

(Eric Bentley, 1946, in Ellmann, p. 112)

'*The Importance of Being Earnest* is his supreme demolition of late nineteenth-century social and moral attitudes, the triumphal conclusion to his career as revolutionary moralist. ... What is wrong

with this society, so the farce implies, is its fatal
inability to distinguish between the trivial and the
serious. Sense and nonsense, reason and fantasy,
facts and truth, are juggled with, forcing new
perspectives, offering release from the cramp of
habit and logic.'

(Katherine Worth, 1980, pp. 155–156)

'Realism is only a background; it cannot form an
artistic motive for a play that is to be a work of art.'

(Wilde, 1895, in Tydeman, p. 41)

'You see that the conduct of the people in itself is
rational enough; it is exquisitely irrational in the
circumstances. Their motives, too, are quite rational
in themselves; they are only irrational as being fitted
to the wrong set of actions. And the result is that
you have something like real life in detail, yet, in
sum, absolutely unlike it; the familiar materials of
life shaken up, as it were, and rearranged in strange,
unreal patterns.'

(A.B. Walkely, 1895, in Beckson, p. 199)

'Shaw found the play "inhuman" and, of course, in
a sense, he was right: Wilde's whole art is calculated
to prevent his characters becoming people.'

(Ian Gregor, 1966, in Tydeman, p. 122)

'... in *The Importance of Being Earnest* Wilde
succeeded ... in writing what is perhaps the only
pure verbal opera in English. The solution that,
deliberately or accidentally, he found was to
subordinate every other dramatic element to
dialogue for its own sake and create a verbal
universe in which the characters are determined by

the kinds of things they say, and the plot is nothing
but a succession of opportunities to say them.'
(W.H. Auden, 1963, in Ellmann, p. 136)

'[Wilde] keeps our attention … on the language,
rather than on the pure comedy of situation. Farce
in Wilde is always shaped and controlled by
precision of language, and it is this which
distinguishes it from farce in general, which is
shaped by arbitrariness of event.'
(Ian Gregor, 1966, in Tydeman, p. 124)

◆ *Activities*

1 Consider whether the play presents some moral evaluation
of characters' behaviour.

a Arrange the characters on a scale of moral worth, from the
most admirable character to the least.

b What criteria would you use for such an evaluation?

2 *The Importance of Being Earnest* is a comedy. It is studied
in schools, colleges and universities because it is seen, by
most audiences and readers, as a very funny play.

   If a theatre director were to stage the play today, what
aspects of the comedy would s/he emphasise to make it
appeal to a modern student audience?

3 Imagine that you were asked to produce the programme
notes for a modern production of *The Importance of Being
Earnest*, aimed at a student audience. Write these notes,
drawing on any of the critical readings above to help you.

4 How rich a resource is *The Importance of Being Earnest* for
finding out about life in late nineteenth-century England?

   Working with other students, collect quotations from the
play that tell you how affluent people lived in the 1890s.
You could create a collage of quotations under various
headings: education, servants, the Church, transport, food

and drink, entertainment, politics, money, marriage, romance, clothes, death.

5 What do you think would be gained and lost by an all-male production of *The Importance of Being Earnest* and/or an all-female one?

6 Anthony Asquith's film version of the play looks mostly like a stage production. Choose a short scene and write a film version in which the camera directs quite definitely what the audience sees.

◆

GLOSSARY

11 **Half-Moon Street:** a fashionable address, near Park Lane

12 **refreshment at five o'clock:** In upper-class society tea would be a substantial meal, with dinner at about 8.30 p.m.

16 **Tunbridge Wells:** a spa town in Kent, traditionally associated with aged, respectable people

19 **Willis's:** a fashionable restaurant, near the St James's theatre

   sent down: A man would accompany a woman from the drawing room to the dining room and then sit with her for the meal.

20 **Wagnerian:** Richard Wagner (1813–1883). His operas frequently offer roles for female singers with very powerful voices.

29 **duties exacted from one after one's death:** Death duties (a tax on inherited wealth) were introduced in the 1894 Government budget.

30 **Liberal Unionist:** Led by Joseph Chamberlain (1836–1914), the Unionists defected from the Liberal Party over Prime Minister Gladstone's proposals for Irish Home Rule. They formed a coalition government with the Conservatives in 1895.

31 **cloak-room:** the left-luggage room

   social indiscretion: an illegitimate baby

   the season: the traditional time for announcing engagements to be married

32 **Gorgon:** (in Greek mythology) three monstrous sisters who had snakes for hair and whose gaze turned to stone anyone who looked at them

34 **eighteen:** the age at which upper-class girls entered 'society' and became marriageable

35 **Club:** one of the exclusively male clubs in London

   Empire: a famous music-hall in Leicester Square

40 **Mudie:** a London circulating library – books were sent to subscribers

41   **abandoned:** This has a double meaning: mislaid or forsaken, but also sexually uninhibited, hence Cecily's response.

        Chasuble: A chasuble is a vestment worn by priests.

42   **Egeria:** a mythological nymph who advised Numa Pompilius, the second king of Rome

        Laetitia: Latin for happiness

45   **Quixotic:** pursuing lofty but unattainable ideals, from *Don Quixote*, a satire on chivalric romances by Miguel de Cervantes (1547–1616)

        Maréchal Niel: a yellow rose

46   **scholar's shudder:** provoked by Miss Prism's neologism 'womanthrope' formed from both Old English and Greek roots

        Primitive: early Christian

48   **manna:** (in the Old Testament) food miraculously provided for the Israelites (Exodus, 16)

        thrift: economical management, but used here as a euphemism for controlling sexual desire

52   **dressing-case:** a case which contained such items as hair brushes, razors, etc.

        dog-cart: a small carriage for carrying hunting dogs

56   **14th of February:** St Valentine's day and also the date of the play's first performance

74   **German scepticism:** In philosophy, sceptics do not believe that absolute truth can be attained; such scepticism was a strong element in German philosophy, especially that of Arthur Schopenhauer (1788–1860).

76   **luggage train:** a goods train

77   **N.B.:** North Britain, an alternative term for Scotland

78   **Funds:** government stocks

81   **Oxonian:** a graduate of Oxford University

        Perrier-Jouet, Brut, '89: a dry champagne, considered a particularly good vintage

84   **Anabaptists:** a Protestant movement which believed that adults should be re-baptised

85   **bassinet:** a pram

87   **Gower Street:** location of the British Museum and London University

Leamington: a spa town and, like Tunbridge Wells, associated with respectable, old people

to cast a stone: In the Bible, stoning was the punishment for adultery.

FURTHER READING

Other works

Oscar Wilde's complete writings amount to only about 1200 pages in the Collins edition. Compared with many nineteenth-century writers, it is not a huge task to read everything he wrote. The following short list is a starting-point to show the range of the writing:

One of the three social comment plays:
Lady Windermere's Fan (1892)
A Woman of No Importance (1893)
An Ideal Husband (1895)

The Picture of Dorian Gray (1890: a novel)

The Selfish Giant (1888: a children's story)

De Profundis (1905: an autobiography; full version 1949)

The Ballad of Reading Gaol (1898: a poem)

'The Critic as Artist' (1890: an essay)

Biography

Richard Ellmann, *Oscar Wilde* (Penguin, 1988)

Rupert Hart-Davis (ed.), *Selected Letters of Oscar Wilde* and *More Letters of Oscar Wilde* (Oxford University Press, 1979 and 1985)

Juliet Gardiner, *Oscar Wilde A Life in Letters, Writings and Wit* (Collins & Brown, 1995); an illustrated biography.

Criticism

Peter Raby (ed.), *The Cambridge Companion to Oscar Wilde* (Cambridge University Press, 1997); a wide-ranging collection of essays, offering some of the latest thinking about Wilde, the context of his time and his influence.

Karl Beckson (ed.), *Oscar Wilde: The Critical Heritage* (Routledge and Kegan Paul, 1970); some later essays but mainly useful for contemporary reviews.

Richard Ellmann (ed.), *Oscar Wilde: A Collection of Critical Essays* (Prentice Hall, 1969)

William Tydeman (ed.), *Wilde, Comedies: A Selection of Critical Essays* (Macmillan, 1982)

Katherine Worth, *Oscar Wilde* (Macmillan, 1980); deals only with Wilde as a dramatist – a clear, straightforward introduction to reading criticism.

Film

The Importance of Being Earnest (1952), directed by Anthony Asquith, is available on video. Excellent cast, including Edith Evans' legendary portrayal of Lady Bracknell.

Wilde (1997) stars Stephen Fry as Wilde and is a very moving account of his marriage and subsequent obsession with Lord Alfred Douglas.

The Trials of Oscar Wilde (1960) has an excellent performance by Peter Finch as Wilde.

Audio

The Importance of Being Earnest features Greg Wide and Miriam Margolyes (Penguin Audio Books).

Great Trials: Oscar Wilde: Compiled from the transcripts of the trials by Gyles Brandreth and performed by Martin Jarvis.

CAMBRIDGE LITERATURE

Ben Jonson   *The Alchemist*

William Wycherley   *The Country Wife*

Robert Burns   *Selected Poems*

William Blake   *Selected Works*

Jane Austen   *Pride and Prejudice*

Jane Austen   *Emma*

Mary Shelley   *Frankenstein*

Three Victorian Poets

Charlotte Brontë   *Jane Eyre*

Emily Brontë   *Wuthering Heights*

Nathaniel Hawthorne   *The Scarlet Letter*

Charles Dickens   *Hard Times*

Charles Dickens   *Great Expectations*

George Eliot   *Silas Marner*

Thomas Hardy   *Far from the Madding Crowd*

Henrik Ibsen   *A Doll's House*

Robert Louis Stevenson   *Treasure Island*

Mark Twain   *Huckleberry Finn*

Thomas Hardy   *Tess of the d'Urbervilles*

Oscar Wilde   *The Importance of Being Earnest*

Kate Chopin   *The Awakening and other stories*

Anton Chekhov   *The Cherry Orchard*

Edith Wharton   *Ethan Frome*

James Joyce   *Dubliners*

Six Poets of the Great War

D. H. Lawrence   *Selected Short Stories*

Edith Wharton   *The Age of Innocence*

F. Scott Fitzgerald   *The Great Gatsby*

Virginia Woolf   *A Room of One's Own*

Robert Cormier   *After the First Death*

Caryl Churchill   *The After-Dinner Joke*
and *Three More Sleepless Nights*

Graham Swift   *Learning to Swim*

Fay Weldon   *Letters to Alice*

Louise Lawrence   *Children of the Dust*

Julian Barnes   *A History of the World in 10½ Chapters*

Amy Tan   *The Joy Luck Club*

Four Women Poets

Moments of Madness – *150 years of short stories*

Helen Edmundson   *The Mill on the Floss*